The Postmodern Parish

New Ministry for a New Era

JIM KITCHENS

THE
ALBAN
INSTITUTE

Library of Congress Control Number 2003112707

ISBN 1-56699-280-X

07 06 05 04 03 VG 1 2 3 4 5 6 7 8 9 10

The
Postmodern
Parish

CONTENTS

108485

A Seismic Shift

I was preaching in Alaska in a small congregation in Homer when, in the middle of my sermon, the earth began to shake, the light fixtures swayed, the glass rattled. It took me about three seconds to realize that I was in my first ever earthquake. I was unnerved to say the least. I gulped, stopped mid-sentence, grasped the edge of the pulpit, and prayed for it to end. Fortunately for my nerves, the tremor lasted only a couple of seconds. But I was thoroughly shaken. It's no small thing for the first time in your life to feel the earth move beneath your feet, the walls shake, and the church threaten to come unglued.

Yet the earthquake was not as unnerving to me as the reaction of those Alaska Methodists to the earthquake. In my momentary terror I looked out at them and they just sat there, unmoved, unruffled, and unperturbed. What for me was a near-death experience was for them just another day in Alaska.

"Last time two of those light fixtures fell," laconically commented one of them. That was it. I'm sure this is a prejudiced comment of a flatlander who is unaccustomed to the heaving Alaskan terrain, but still, something just doesn't seem right about a congregation that's able to stay serene during an earthquake. When the earth heaves and the ground shifts beneath our feet, I want a church that's screaming and ducking under the pews.

Stanley Hauerwas and I began our book *Resident Aliens: Life in the Christian Colony* with a claim that a "seismic shift" had occurred in American church life. The ground had shifted under our feet, great rifts had split the earth down the middle, tall buildings were crashing, and yet too many of us in the church were trying to sleep through an earthquake. We dated this earthshaking event as the 1960 opening of the Fox Movie Theater on Sunday in defiance of the state's laws against movies on Sunday, but we could have used other examples. The old, comfortable, Constantinian arrangement between the church and the world, the mainline Protestant hegemony over American life, the alliance between Christians and culture was ending. Hauerwas and I thought that it was high time for the church to wake up and get with the earthquake. Church as usual, ministry as we have always done it, just won't get the job done. We've got to realize that the ground beneath our feet has shifted and that the church is being given a new mission to a changed world. Start screaming.

Which goes a long way to explain why I am so excited about Jim Kitchens's *The Emerging Church*. Kitchens stands on tiptoes on the horizon and envisions a new church, re-formed and ever reforming, a church with a future that draws upon our New Testament, missional past and boldly embodies the gospel. Here is a hopeful, practical, visionary book. If you have tired, as have I, of how-to cookbooks that promise a quick fix for a church in trouble, if you have despaired of programs for church self-aggrandizement that build more on the razzle-dazzle of Wall Street and Madison Avenue advertising gurus than the biblical faith delivered to the saints, I think you will like Kitchens's perspective.

Here is portrayed a church waiting to be born. It is emerging, not yet here, but already on the way. An earthquake, to extend my metaphor, is both a sign of an old world that's coming apart and a new world that is being born. An old world breaks open, shakes, falls down, gives way so that a new world might emerge. Some of us in the church today still feel some grief and dismay that our old world, the one we thought we knew how to work to the advantage of the gospel, is receding. Kitchens candidly acknowledges the losses we are suffering. Having once been culturally significant, American churches are feeling sidelined in a postmodern, post-Christian world. We are feeling more like strangers in the very culture we thought we owned.

Yet by God's grace a new world is emerging. Something is dying, yes, but something is also being born. Kitchens points us toward that new world. He takes a vast amount of thinking that has been going on about our once and future church, thinking by some of our most faithful and creative church observers and theologians, and boils it down into accessible, practical, workable guidance for pastors and church leaders who want their congregations to be part of God's movements in our time. Therefore this book would be great for study at a church leaders' retreat, or at a pastors' conference, or by any person or among any group that wants the old church to be part of the new church. Kitchens will show you how not to be left behind by the emerging church. If you have been dismayed, depressed, and discouraged by the present state of your church, Kitchens can show you what to do today in order to get to where you know Jesus intends his Body to be tomorrow. His analysis of our postmodern situation, his stress on the missional vocation of the church, his emphasis on worship and the theological purposes of the church enable us to see the horizon as a gift of God rather than nuisance and crisis for the church. Stop screaming and start rebuilding.

As Matthew tells his story of the Easter, when the faithful women come to the tomb, early in the morning, a great stone sealed the tomb where the body of Jesus lay. Pilate wanted to be sure that the crucified, dead Jesus stayed that way. Suddenly, there was a great earthquake (Matthew 28:2). The stone was rolled away. Jesus was loose.

See? Earthquakes can be good. Sign of new life, the break of a new day, the emerging body of Christ sallying forth from death and entombment, come, Risen Lord Jesus, shake us, rattle and roll us, raise us up!

William H. Willimon
Dean of the Chapel and
    Professor of Christian Ministry
Duke Divinity School
Pentecost, 2003

PREFACE

Long before I ever read an article containing the word "postmodern" or "gen X," I knew a seismic change was underway in the context in which I served as pastor. The pieces no longer fit. Old ways of doing ministry no longer worked. Things were inexplicably out of joint.

Perhaps I intuited this shift early on in my ministry because the first two parishes I served were in California—one in downtown Oakland and the other in the university community of Davis. Congregations on the West Coast have long understood that they no longer have the broad cultural support that the American church of the 1950s enjoyed. They don't necessarily know what to *do* about their social dislocation, but at least they've been conscious of it for at least a generation. They also understand that the broader culture around them has undergone major changes in the past 40 years. This double awareness has given them the opportunity to get a head start on struggling with the waves of cultural change now crashing in on congregations throughout America.

Whether young or old, today's pastors are going to be blessed (or cursed, depending on your point of view) with the call to wrestle with these cultural shifts and their implications for ministry. None of us is going to be able to come to terms fully with this new setting for ministry before we pass from the scene. Like it or not, we are *always* going to be living with questions about how, in a continually shifting cultural landscape, to make our ministries faithful.

Much of what has been written about these cultural changes—and especially about postmodernism in particular—

has concentrated on what church leaders ought to *think* or to *say* in response. The focus has been on preaching and apologetics. In this book, however, I focus more on how the church ought to *live* in response to our changed cultural setting: how worship, Christian formation, mission, and leadership need to change if our congregations are going to embody the gospel faithfully in a postmodern world.

I also mean for the title of this book, *The Postmodern Parish*, to indicate that my focus is on what many of us refer to as "parish ministry," rather than on the specialized ministries to which many faithful ordained clergy commit themselves, or on the ministries of larger church judicatories. The term "parish" may no longer have the same geographic connotations it had in earlier American church history (and still does, to an extent, in the Roman Catholic tradition). It may now be defined more by our denominational heritage or our location along the theological spectrum. But most of us still have a sense of what we mean by the term: that particular local Christian community we are called to serve.

In addition, much of what has been written about our postmodern, postdenominational, and post-Christian setting for ministry (the three "posts" on which I will focus) has been written by evangelicals. Many mainline pastors have picked up such books but have found it difficult to work through the evangelical mind-set and vocabulary to uncover the author's insights. I hope that by writing about these issues from a mainline perspective I will make it easier for other mainline pastors and church leaders to get to the meat of what I have to offer.

What follows is not meant to be a blueprint for congregational change that can be replicated in any mainline parish. Instead, I offer it as one pastor's and one congregation's experience in trying to wrestle faithfully with the challenges our new cultural context presents. I hope that by reading this book you, in turn, will be encouraged to grapple with these changes in ways that have integrity for you and for the congregation you lead. The more of us who engage in this process of discernment, the more quickly and clearly we will be able to see the shape of a church that will be faithful in this new landscape—what I call "the emerging church."

As this book nears publication, I am undergoing a time of transition myself, leaving the congregation I have served for more than 15 years and moving into a new pastoral call and, thus, into a different cultural context for discerning the shape of the emerging church. I now have the opportunity to wrestle with these changes in a new setting and with a new set of conversation partners. The process of discernment continues.

Acknowledgments

As I indicate throughout this book, discerning the shape of the emerging church is not a solitary project. This discernment requires colleagues—both personal and institutional—who share in the process. I want to thank the many people and communities who have been those colleagues for me.

First, I want to thank the congregation and the leadership of Davis Community Church, Davis, California, for their desire to listen for the guidance of the Holy Spirit, their openness to experiment with change, and their willingness to trust their pastors' intuitions. In particular I want to thank the church's session (governing board) for the sabbatical it granted me, which gave me time to reflect on what we had learned together over the preceding 14 years. In this same context, I also want to thank the Center of Theological Inquiry (CTI) in Princeton, New Jersey, and its director, Wallace Alston, for inviting me to be pastor-theologian in residence at the center during that sabbatical, providing a space in which this book could begin to take shape.

I want to thank the colleagues in groups that, over the years, have prodded me to read broadly and think critically as I have served in parish ministry, and that have encouraged me in the Reformed emphasis on the life of the mind in the service of God: the Wednesday Ministers' Study Group, which has gathered for study and support in Piedmont, California, for more than 25 years; the Western Regional collegium of CTI's Pastor-Theologian program; the group of Presbyterian pastors pulled together by Laird Stuart and Jack Haberer to build friendships across lines of disagreement in our denomination; and the members of the Dead Theologians' Society in Sacramento, California.

I am deeply indebted to mentors who have acknowledged my gifts and urged their development along the way of my ministry: the late Mort McMillan, my pastor in Tupelo, Mississippi, at the time I decided to go to seminary; John Turpin, my pastoral colleague in Oakland, California, who became (and remains) my primary mentor and dear friend; Joe Small of the Office of Theology and Worship staff at the Presbyterian Center in Louisville; and Wallace Alston of CTI, who invited me into wider circles of conversation in the church.

I want to thank James Wind and Gil Rendle of the Alban Institute for encouraging me to submit my work for publication. I have also been greatly aided in preparing my manuscript by Alban editors Beth Gaede and Jean Caffey Lyles. They helped me discover what I still remember from the efforts of all my English teachers (and what I have woefully forgotten). What you read in this book will be much clearer and more focused because of their critical eyes and gentle suggestions.

I cannot say enough to convey how much my colleagues in ministry at Davis Community Church—and especially Mary Lynn Tobin, my co-pastor, and Sandra Lommasson, director of our Bread of Life Center for Christian Formation—have meant to me both personally and professionally. I have been graced to have great colleagues who just happen also to be great friends. Our mutual commitment to listening to the leadership of the Spirit has been one of the greatest joys in my ministry. They have been my chief conversation partners as I've grown as a pastor, and they have invested much time and love into encouraging me to grow as a child of God.

Finally, and most profoundly, I want to thank my wife, Deborah, and my daughters, Sara and Jessica, for their love and support over the years. Their willingness to "share" me with the congregations I have served and their unfailing ability to pull me off any high horse upon which I have managed to set myself, and to remind me that I'm a frail and funny human being as well as a pastor, have not only kept me sane but also reminded me to rely always on God's grace. Anything good I have learned about how to be a caring pastor and loving person, I learned first from them.

The
Postmodern
Parish

CHAPTER 1

A New Context
for Ministry

Many of us who serve as pastors of mainline local churches have long felt that something is amiss in the life of our congregations. It's hard to name exactly what is wrong, but occasionally we have a nagging sense that something is just not working anymore. Our best hunch is that the "disconnect" is not rooted within us. Rather, it feels as though the cultural gestalt has shifted in the external context for ministry. Our best efforts at ministry seem to be about a half-beat behind some new pulse that is beginning to course through the culture.

Whether we're baby boomer or generation X pastors, we're aware that the ground rules for being an American are changing beneath us, that something fundamental about the way we have lived as Christian communities in the recent past no longer works. This tectonic shift in the cultural context of ministry renders our attempts to patch up our congregation's ministries notably unsatisfying—both for our members and for us.

Boomer pastors tend to replicate patterns of parish life learned from predecessors, but boomers sense that these patterns are becoming dried-out husks, with the vitality hollowed out of them—vitality they possessed when boomers first entered ministry. Christian education programs that seemed exciting and innovative 10 years ago now fall flat and listless. Outreach and evangelism ministries that once renewed people's faith now leave them disenchanted, uninterested, or burned out. We wonder whether people are

finding more meaningful fellowship in civic clubs and com-
puter chat rooms than in the church. The liturgical renewal
movement, which was invigorating many a mainline church
as we began our ministries, appears to have run out of steam,
having devolved into "worship wars," in which the arms
borne into battle are pipe organs and praise bands.

Pastors who are gen X or younger wonder why congregations and church boards don't "get" that the culture has
radically changed. We puzzle over why older members want
to hold on to forms of church life that may have inspired
them when they were young, but that do not meet the needs
of today's 20-somethings. And even when a board admits
that some of its congregation's cherished forms of church
life are on their last legs, they still fear to experiment. We feel
as if we're beating our heads against an invisible wall, trying
to help our congregations understand that if they want to
remain healthy, they must be open to change. We're not even
sure how to help them understand that change is part of the
natural life cycle in a church, as it is in any living thing.

Observing the decline of vitality in our congregations,
we've tried everything we can imagine to pump new life
into them, but with meager results. We buy everything the
Alban Institute or church-change gurus Bill Easum and Lyle
Schaller put out; we read books by "successful" pastors, even
if we disagree with their theology; and we give every seminar and programmatic "fix" on the market a shot. We pray
there's a ministry resource that—if we can just find it—will
fix everything that's wrong in our congregation's life.

We are desperate for insight. No matter what we do, however, we still feel that something fundamental is amiss. Something more foundational is happening in the church and the
culture.

Three Clues to Our Situation

Three adjectives that pop up regularly in the books and articles we read, as we search for that magical silver bullet,
point in the direction of this more fundamental shift:

postmodern, post-Christian, and *postdenominational.* Most of us have a good sense of what it means to live in a "modern" world shaped by Enlightenment thought forms. We know that the culture in which we grew up has been foundationally shaped by Western Christian values. We appreciate the denominational tradition that shaped us. We also have at least some understanding of what the "post" prefix usually means. By postmodernism, we mean that people lack the kind of faith in science they had a generation ago, look more to unmediated experience than to rational thought to give meaning to their lives, and doubt that one single metanarrative can explain the world. In using "post-Christian," we acknowledge a growing awareness that Christianity doesn't have nearly the degree of broad cultural influence in America that it once had. That we now inhabit a post-denominational setting is signaled by how much less "brand loyalty" Christians show as they move easily from one denominational tradition to another. We can no longer assume that everyone sees the world the way most Americans did even 30 years ago. We'll explore each of these "posts" in more detail below, but even this brief sketch helps give shape and form to what we already know about the changes American culture is undergoing. And it helps us begin to understand that we're going to have to shape a different sort of church if we're going to be faithful to the gospel in this new cultural setting.

We really don't have much choice about whether we are going to deal with these changes: the train has already left the station! But we do have a choice about *how* we will deal with them. We can adopt a whole range of strategies—from deciding to make wrestling with the meaning of this shift a cornerstone of our ministries to ignoring the cultural changes altogether and doing ministry just as we have in the past. Our choices are analogous to the choices you have when you wade into a powerful ocean surf. You can face into the waves as they come toward shore and make a conscious decision to jump over them, dive under them, or dig in your heels as they wash over you. Or you can stand with your back to the waves, ignoring them, and run the (highly likely) risk that eventually a wave will come along that is powerful enough to knock you down and drag you under. The truth of the matter is that the waves are headed toward shore no matter which direction you choose to face. The difference in how they will affect you is based on whether you choose to plunge into them or ignore them.

Any *one* of these cultural shifts would have a major impact on the way we do ministry as we enter the 21st century. But *all three* cultural waves are crashing onto the shore of congregational life at the same time, each magnifying the impact of the other two. We're not just looking at gentle waves lapping onto that shore, then. We're dealing with a tsunami!

I will say more about each of these three developments in the sections that follow. Later chapters will address in more detail how these contextual shifts invite us to change the way we think about and act in particular arenas of congregational life: worship, Christian formation, mission, and leadership.

Postmodernity

We already know that postmodernism is going to have a deep impact on Western culture in the century that lies before us. There's no way that parish pastors can yet fully understand its impact, though, because even academics aren't sure exactly what they mean by the term.

The term "postmodern" points toward a cluster of related emphases in the academy, depending on whether one is applying it in literature, architecture, or theology (and academics are only *beginning* to sense what it might mean to talk about postmodern chemistry or physics).

People using the term "postmodern" are pointing out a change in cultural self-awareness that challenges the basic assumptions underlying what some philosophers and sociologists refer to as "the modern experiment"—that way of understanding the world born out of the Enlightenment and systematized through the rise of empirical science. Many of the philosophical foundations for this modern experiment—

for example, a trust in rationality, a discounting of the intuitive or miraculous, a primacy placed on the individual rather than on the group—have been roundly challenged in recent years. More radical critics of modernity are not so much proposing a new set of foundations to replace those of modernity as they are challenging the whole idea of "foundationalism," challenging the proposition that there can be *any* universal foundation for constructing a common view of the world. More humble postmodern theorists say that postmodernity is little more than modernity's becoming critically aware of itself, coming to understand that modernity is but another in a long line of cultural constructs that, after an era of domination, slowly fade from the scene.

Four Evidences of a Postmodern World

It would take a substantial library to lay out the philosophical underpinnings of postmodernism. However, in a pamphlet titled "The End of the Modern World," published by the Center of Theological Inquiry in Princeton, New Jersey, Princeton Seminary philosopher Diogenes Allen suggests four ways in which the breakdown of the modern world is most evident.[1] Perhaps that would be a good place for us to begin:

> *Modernity's claim that we live in a self-contained universe is no longer believable.*

Modernity sought to build a model of the universe that would require no "outside" causes, especially not a transcendent God who "stands" outside the world. More recently, however, natural scientists themselves—especially in the fields of cosmology and subatomic physics—have begun to open the door to the possibility that the universe may well *not* be self-contained. (Even the latter-day deist and cosmologist Stephen Hawking admits that God might be behind the Big Bang, though he doesn't see how God would need to *continue* to be involved in the life of a universe fully determined by natural scientific laws, once the "t=0" moment was over.)

We can now speak of God in a cultural context that grants a far more open-minded hearing to the assertion of God's continuing, active involvement in the life of the world than it received when scientists felt they had eliminated the need of God as an explanatory cause.

Modernity failed to find a basis for morality and society in reason (rather than God).

One of the great experiments of the modern era was the attempt, exemplified by the work of philosopher Immanuel Kant, to find a foundation for morality in human reason alone, without recourse to a transcendent God. Postmodern deconstructionists like Jacques Derrida, though, have radically critiqued Kant's attempt, contending that his is nothing more than yet another in a long line of attempts by the powerful to assert their power by defining the meaning of the culture and the relationships within it. Their critique undermines the Kantian confidence in human reason as the sole basis for ethics and gives the church a wider public hearing for its proclamation that God's self-revelation provides a better (even the true?) basis for morality. A 1989 *Atlantic Monthly* article by sociologist Glenn Tinder, "Can We Be Good Without God?,"[2] makes the case that, absent some transcendent anchor point, a system of morality cannot be defended as superior to any proffered alternative. But if no system can be shown to be superior, we are inevitably led to that popular caricature of postmodern thinking, "It's all relative." If we construct our morality along only the horizontal plane—relying only on human reason and refusing to involve any transcendent referent—that system of morality, in the end, will becomes a Nietzschean power play. Whoever gets to determine the rules in a language game (especially in morality) is most likely to "win." The breakdown of the hegemony of Kantian thought opens the debate about ethics in postmodernism to a whole range of perspectives, from a rampant relativism to an approach rooted in a transcendent God.

The end of the modern era has led to a collapse in the belief in inevitable progress.

Part of the hubris of the natural sciences, at least in their modernist form, was their belief that scientists had the tools needed to overcome all problems facing humankind. The horrors of World War I effectively punctured the belief in inevitable progress, but it has taken until the end of the 20th century for us to comprehend fully that scientific advancement will not lead us to a utopia. Indeed, it is possible that 500 years hence, people will look back on the four to five centuries that followed the Enlightenment as an incredibly naïve time during which humanity thought it had gained mastery over nature. Developments like the appearance of "superbug" bacteria resistant to all antibiotics and our continuing failure to eradicate war as a means of diplomacy are evidence that such mastery remains elusive and that progress in human affairs is *not* inevitable. Losing their "faith" in science may, in new ways, open people to the church's message that meaning in human life is to be found in relationship to God, not in science's solving all our ills.

The postmodern critique of modernity challenges its assumption that knowledge is inherently good.

"If it can be done, it should be done" only slightly caricatures an axiom employed by some scientists as they seek to understand the physical universe. But we live in a world where nuclear weapons and environmental degradation make us all too aware that potential negative outcomes lurk in the unrestrained pursuit of knowledge. Many Americans worry whether some of our more recent scientific advancements (for example, cloning technology) haven't outstripped our moral capacity to determine whether they ought to be pursued. People are growing more open to a transcendent referent to guide society in its pursuit of knowledge, more open to Paul's insight that "All things are lawful, but not all things are beneficial" (1 Cor. 10:23).

Additional Evidence

Allen gives us a helpful start in defining postmodernism; however, I would expand upon his definition by offering what follows.

> *The dawning of the postmodern era is accompanied by a healing of the modernist rift between the natural sciences and theology.*

One way to "graph" the course of the modern era is to plot the growing separation between the trajectories of theology and the natural sciences, beginning with the rise of empirical science. During the modern era, the natural sciences tended to usurp theology's role as "queen of the sciences," so that we have grown up in an era when "proving something scientifically" has been the most important way of confirming a truth claim's veracity. The rise of logical positivism in the early part of the 20th century provided a philosophical basis for dividing knowledge into two realms: the sciences, which were about "facts" that could be publicly tested, and theology, which was about "values" that were private and, therefore, unverifiable. One change in the way scientists now understand their own work, stemming from the application of quantum mechanics and Heisenberg's uncertainty principle, is their realization that there is no such thing as an "uninterpreted fact." Every "fact" is influenced, however slightly, by the particular scientific theory with which you are working when you assert that datum. This insight has led a number of philosophers of science to conclude that there is not really as significant a difference as both fields formerly asserted between the truth claims scientists make and the truth claims of theologians. The current dialogue between theology and the natural sciences is exploring how God's self-revelation in Torah or Jesus, for example, can, as truly as laboratory experiments, help us to understand the way the world "really is." The church no longer has to labor with the burden of trying to make the content of its proclamation verifiable by the scientific method, or "rationally" explaining anything that might raise a scientist's eyebrows (for example, special revelation, miracles, the resurrection of the body). We are set free from the ways in which we have self-censored our theology in the recent past—free to proclaim our tradition in its fullness. We are also set free to ask difficult questions of natural scientists from the perspective of faith, in the way that we have been accustomed to their asking difficult questions of us from the perspective of science. Reason and revelation no longer have to be an "either-or" option, but can be understood as complementary ways of discovering God's truth.

The decline of the modern era is accompanied by a waning in the emphasis on the individual.

One mark of the modern era was its elevation of the individual over the community. Jews and Christians proclaim that each individual is a child of God and infinitely precious in the Creator's sight. However, both traditions have rooted the value of the individual in one's being a member of the Jewish nation or of the body of Christ, part of a larger community to which one is accountable. The modernist emphasis on the individual has manifested itself differently in mainline congregations, depending on whether they are liberal or evangelical. Liberal congregations have tended to emphasize relational or sexual freedom; evangelical congregations, economic or political freedom. Nonetheless, all have tended to emphasize the individual's desires over the needs of the community. That emphasis came home to me during a congregational forum at our church. A member addressing the congregation repeated a statement many of us heard in the abortion debates of the 1970s: "It's my body, and no one can tell me what to do with it." Instinctively, I knew her argument was deeply at odds with a biblical understanding of community. It was *not* just her body, but a body connected to a larger community, and the woman was accountable to that community. The decision was *not* hers alone to make; nor would she be the only person in the community to bear the consequences of her choice. The hyperindividualism she inherited from late modernity in America warped her distinctively Christian understanding of community. Modernity's emphasis on individualism also tends to distort our appreciation of all communal polities, from the family to the nation-state. By placing a greater emphasis on balancing the individual with the communal, postmodernism will help Christians to reassert those resources within the tradition that balance our "rights" as individuals with our responsibilities to one another as members of the body of Christ.

Postmodernism helps us see the continuing value of ways to define the world that are rooted in the narratives of particular traditions.

During the 20th century, modernist modes of thought persuaded many of us of the need to translate the peculiar language and worldview embodied in scripture into what late modernity deemed the more "universal" languages of psychology and sociology—those fields in which the Kantian experiment was popularly continued. Here we came as close as we ever have to selling our birthright to modernity for a mess of pottage. I remember a running argument I had for seven years with an elder in a congregation I previously served. He kept after me to translate the "strange terms" of the gospel and Christian tradition into "language that ordinary folks would understand." Inevitably, what he meant was that I should translate terms like "grace" into what he thought were their psychological cognates. I argued that we should instead be inviting nonbelievers to come to our worship services long enough to learn the particular meaning of "grace" in the Christian tradition: to hear enough stories about God's grace, to participate often enough in its ritual enactment, and to experience God's grace in confession and reconciliation sufficiently that a sense of the term's Christian meaning would begin to grow in them. I still think I took the right side of that argument. However, if you ask the average group of Christians today to talk about their faith, you'll find, more often than not, that they use far more therapeutic than theological language. Again, this will be truer of liberal Christians than of evangelical ones, but true of all nonetheless. Postmodern philosophers of language help us understand that there *is* no universal human language set, but that every language set asserts a unique way of seeing the world. This insight sets us free to embrace, without apology, the particular language of scripture and tradition, to mine it for its singular riches, and to enculturate our people into the unique worldview formed by its vocabulary, grammar, and syntax. Of course, the language set provided by scripture and tradition will necessarily be shaped by the time and the place in which we live. But postmodern philosophers give us a platform from which to proclaim again our belief that our tradition conveys a self-revelation of God that can also transcend the particular culture and age in which we receive that revelation.

> *Postmodern people experience life in a far more holistic way than simply through their rationality.*

Rationalism is one of the hallmarks of the Enlightenment and of the modern era that emerged from it. This reliance on reason was bolstered by an Enlightenment emphasis on the value of written texts. For many in the West, this reliance has led almost completely to a "head" religion, one in which thinking about the faith is the central focus of faith, to the disregard of religious experience or feeling. The postmodern collapse of reliance on reason alone gives rise to people who want to engage their senses and their intuition as well as their reason when they encounter God. They want to "taste and see that the Lord is good" (Ps. 34:8)—and hear and smell and touch as well. They are searching for liturgy that involves the body, the heart, and the spirit—*as well as* the mind—in the praise of God. They want to feel as well as think about their Savior. They are open to mystery as well as to explanation. They are deeply hungry for an experience of God's transcendence as well as of God's immanence.

Clearly, postmodern modes of thought are far more complex and nuanced than the outline I have laid out with the help of Diogenes Allen's introduction to his book. What I have outlined, however, is more than sufficient to enable us to grasp that the context for ministry has radically changed beneath us, shifting in a direction that can make us far more confident to proclaim the gospel without feeling the need to accommodate it to "modern, scientific" ways of thinking. We have been set free to encounter the "strange new world within the Bible" into which Karl Barth invited us.

Indeed, postmodernism helps us to understand that, as ethicist Stanley Hauerwas of Duke Divinity School puts it, after a few centuries in which the culture at large snuggled up to the church and was its ally in forming a least-common-denominator sort of civic faith in its citizens, the world has gone back to being the world. While we may initially hear this word as bad news, Hauerwas insists it is good news in that it gives us permission (not that we ever really needed it) to go back to being the church, to being a human community shaped by the particular worldview of scripture.

Post-Christendom

It will come as no surprise to anyone in parish ministry today that American culture no longer actively supports a Christian framework for understanding the world or particular biblical values such as honoring the Sabbath. We encounter this disconnect between religious communities and the wider culture every day.

This lack of cultural support was hammered home to me a few years ago when Independence Day fell on a Sunday. In the community in which I then served as pastor, a local civic club annually sponsored a Fourth of July "kiddie parade," culminating in a family celebration in the city park next to our church. As I entered the pulpit to begin my sermon, the local university band, standing immediately across the street from the pulpit, broke into a spirited rendition of the Eric Clapton tune "Cocaine." No increase in volume on my part (and my parishioners will tell you that I have a rather loud voice) had a prayer of being heard over the band music. Thank goodness, most folk over the age of 70 in the congregation didn't have a clue what the song was about; otherwise, they would have been even more offended than they were already. We muddled through the rest of the service, but I'm not sure how many ears were attuned to the voice of the Spirit that day.

Several aspects of this episode are instructive. First, as the civic club members later confessed, it never entered their minds that a conflict could ensue between their traditional celebration of the Fourth and church services, even though they were clearly aware that July 4 fell on Sunday that year. Secondly, I'm sure no one in the university band's leadership considered the irony that might be perceived by our worshipers when the band played a song about an illicit drug just as their preacher was entering the pulpit. Third, no one in city government gave a second thought to issuing the necessary permits that created the conflict between our congregation's worship and the community's celebration of a civic holiday. The community, which would on the whole be thought of as friendly toward its churches, didn't even have us on its radar screen.

All of us who serve parishes have many stories of this genre in our collection of "can you believe it?" tales about ministry—youth sports team coaches who think nothing of scheduling practices or tournaments on Sunday morning; civic leaders who have no sense of the rhythms of liturgical life in the Christian communities of their towns; teachers and directors who demand that our young people give them greater loyalty than they do their churches. Even harder to take is that many of our own members see their children's participation in parish life as just another of the many options for personal enrichment available to them. How many times do our youth miss involvement in a church activity because of a conflict with ballet class, a language lesson, or a play rehearsal? And with their parents' unreflective approval? At times, it seems as though the church is the only "activity" in town that *doesn't* tell you that you can't play if you miss a practice. Indeed, the sermon that created some of the most negative feedback I've ever received was one in which I made the audacious proposal that participation in church life for children and youth *ought* to be more important than their participation in other community activities!

We forget how deeply steeped in the Christian tradition (or, in some parts of the country, a broader Judeo-Christian tradition) many of our experiences of childhood were, especially if we are boomers or pre-boomers. We forget how important for business and social life it once was for people to know that you were a member in good standing of a religious community. We forget how we used to count on public-school teachers to teach a form of low-church Protestant faith to their students. We forget that a political candidate's religious affiliation always used to be included in the announcement of his or her candidacy. We forget how much more importance parents once put on having their children and youth (and themselves) involved in church life, and how many fewer options vied for the time, energy, and loyalty of our members.

Long gone are the times when you answered roll call in a public school by reciting a Bible verse, sang religious Christmas carols in public-school assemblies, or received a New Testament from the Gideons in your fifth-grade class (all of which were true when I was growing up in Mississippi in the early 1960s). My wife, Deborah, a public-schools administrator, will tell you that doing anything along those lines will get you into far deeper trouble as a teacher than will incompetence or poor classroom management.

Even though we know, at least at an intellectual level, that *everything* has changed in the relationship between the church and the culture in which it lives, we tend to act as if *nothing* had changed. We engage in ministry as if we still expected the culture at large to help us form Christian individuals and Christian community.

Our "Once and Future" Context

But, as Stanley Hauerwas reminds us, the world has gone back to being the world. Rather than supporting the values of the church, American society is, at best, indifferent to and, at worst, slightly hostile toward those values. We can see this change in our congregants' general reluctance to proclaim publicly (i.e., outside the church community) that they are Christian. In part, that reluctance is based on their not wanting to be tarred with the same broad brush with which their fellow citizens paint the televangelists whose sins have brought shame upon the church in the recent past. But that reluctance is even more deeply rooted in their unconscious. They sense that to say one is a Christian in the workplace or in a community organization puts one at some vague interpersonal disadvantage. Or they feel that they would be implying that they are "right" and anyone who believes otherwise is "wrong," thus infringing on everyone's right to a different opinion. Our members also know that the cultural support for being Christian in America today has been seriously eroded.

Alban Institute founder Loren Mead helps us grasp the tenor of this shift when he suggests that the context in which we now minister has more in common with the apostolic era than it has with the church of the 1950s. That is how radically he believes that the context for our ministries has shifted. In his "Once and Future Church" book series Mead proposes that the church is being called upon to learn again how to live in a society whose governmental, economic, and cultural institutions do not necessarily support the church's purposes or share its values and may, in fact, come over time to oppose them.

Now at first this statement does sound like bad news, especially to those of us in the more moderate-to-liberal wing of mainline denominations. We have grown quite used to being invited into the corridors of power, and even to believing that what we said and did there made a difference in how the powerful wielded their power. We've become accustomed to people thinking well of us because we are Christian. We're not prepared to deal with the slightly raised eyebrow at a dinner party in response to our saying we are church members. We are a bit flummoxed by zoning boards that treat our congregations' requests for expansion with no greater deference than they would a request from a downtown business, whereas in the past they would have bent over backward to accommodate our requests. We're puzzled when what we have to say about the "great issues" of the day is of no interest to anyone outside our own sanctuaries.

This is probably the moment in the telling of this tale when our evangelical and Pentecostal brothers and sisters smile and say, "Welcome to the real world." They have never felt similarly close to or accepted by American society. They have rarely been invited into the halls of power (and in the rare exception to this rule—for example Billy Graham's influence with several presidents—they have similarly been corrupted by the experience). Evangelicals have always understood themselves to be countercultural in the sense that they have more consciously espoused distinctive Christian values that they knew to be at odds with the values of the culture at large. Those of us in the more liberal wing of mainline churches have much to learn from our evangelical brothers and sisters about navigating our way through a culture that looks slightly askance at all Christians.

Our Countercultural Existence

Indeed, if there is one lesson that we all—evangelicals and liberals alike—need to learn about the post-Christendom era, it is that we are far more alike than different. While theological issues remain on which we genuinely differ, we need to wake up to the fact that we are one another's only allies against the growing hostility of American culture toward *all* expressions of Christian faith. We'd better start loving one another more and arguing less.

I was holding my usual "office hours" in a local coffee house one morning when an acquaintance from the nearby university sidled up and asked if he could sit and talk with me for a while. He is one of those folk I fondly refer to as "happy pagans"—nice folk, well thought of, "spiritual but not religious," basically good people who would never choose to attend church. As we sipped our cappuccinos, the conversation drifted toward the differences between the Presbyterian congregation I then served (one of the more liberal churches in town) and the fundamentalist Reformed congregation that was usually thought to be at the opposite end of the theological spectrum.

"I don't know why you make such a big deal about how different your two churches are," the happy pagan said to me. "From my perspective, you're pretty much the same. You look at the world the same way. You both think the Bible tells you how you ought to live. You both believe that what happens in history matters in some ultimate sense. You both try to figure out what it means to 'follow Jesus,' which is certainly something different from following Buddha or being a Wiccan."

I went away from that conversation shocked. How in the world could this intelligent person think that the folk at that other church and the members of my congregation were *anything* alike? However, the longer I sat with his comment, the more I became convinced that he was basically right. Both churches wrestled with the same central figure, Jesus Christ. We both turned to the same narrative to interpret the world— the Bible. We both believed that God acts in history and, therefore, that what happens in history matters. Indeed, we both looked at the world through the same lenses, though we might argue about whose prescription for those lenses was just a bit off.

In the decades ahead we will increasingly discover—no matter where on the theological spectrum we find ourselves—that we have far more in common with our brothers and sisters in Christ than we do with those who do not claim him as Lord and Savior. We will increasingly find one another to be allies as we seek to proclaim the faith to an unbelieving world. One of the great challenges before us is whether we can turn our energy from those things that divide us to focus it instead on what unites us in Christ. Can we quit lobbing ideological hand grenades at each other long enough to realize that while we've been arguing with one another the rest of the world has lost interest in what we have to say? Can the centripetal force we have in our unity

in Christ exert a strong enough influence on all of us to overcome the centrifugal force of our theological diversity, which
tends to shatter the body of Christ and scatter its members
in all directions?

Over the past year or so I've had the privilege of being
part of a conversation between pastors on either side of the
debate over the ordination of homosexuals. Over the past
decade or two, this argument has sapped much of the energy in the life of my denomination, the Presbyterian Church
(U.S.A.), as well as in that of many other mainline churches.
We were brought together by a couple of pastors who have
taken leadership roles in that debate, one on either side, but
who have become deeply concerned about voices calling for
a breakup of our denomination—calls from people who have
grown increasingly weary of all the wrangling. The conversation was designed so that we would not talk about homosexuality or ordination directly. Instead we would share
papers and talk about our understanding of more fundamental theological topics, such as the authority of scripture, what
it means to "be saved," and what we think we are saying
when we profess, as we recite the Nicene Creed, that "we
believe in one holy catholic and apostolic church."

The truth is that we began our conversations mistrustful
of one another. After all, the people on the other side of the
table were "them," our opponents on the big issue of the
day. But as we began to share our papers and took the time
to ask each other what was really meant when someone used
a particular word or concept, not only did the mistrust begin
to melt, but also we discovered that we believed pretty much
the same things. Our theologies were not so different after
all. Of course, areas remained where we just had to agree to
disagree, but those points of contention were not central to
our understanding of the Christian faith.

We continue to stand on opposite sides of this one issue.
But through these conversations and the personal relationships that have been established through them, we have discovered that we have much more in common theologically
than what divides us. We have discovered that we all pro-

fess the faith once handed down to the saints and that there are no heretics among us (which is not to say that there are no heretics *anywhere* on the church scene today, just not among this particular set of pastors). We've become more aware of the phrases that unnecessarily trigger disruptive emotional reactions in our opponents and how to say what we believe in ways that don't immediately set people to erecting barricades.

These shared experiences point toward the most important implication of our living in a post-Christian age: those of us who are Christian, while not totally setting aside the important issues on which we disagree, are being called to redirect our energy and our focus toward rediscovering the common faith that sets us apart from the wider American culture and makes us a countercultural sign of the reign of God.

Redirecting this energy will require discipline on the part of all of us. We will be asked to divert the tremendous energy we expend in arguing our favorite divisive issue and to redirect that energy into building up the common faith shared by all. We will need to take on the difficult work of carefully explaining ourselves and our beliefs to one another and of asking thoughtful questions, all the while trusting in our common commitment to the tradition we profess.

Postdenominationalism

I have saved this third "post" till last, because I think postmodern modes of thought and the awareness that we live in a post-Christian era have far greater impact on the life of the church. However, it is important to acknowledge that denominations, whose historical existence parallels that of nation-states (no accident), may be fading in importance in these early years of the 21st century (just as nation-states are starting to give way to a global political community).

I remember being struck by Princeton sociologist Robert Wuthnow's musing that the horizontal line one could draw between liberals and evangelicals in the American church is a more meaningful marker for understanding alliances in today's church than are the vertical lines that divide the church into denominational families. Intuitively, I knew he was right. Indeed, when I think about my own ministry, I realize that I have far more frequent, comfortable, and meaningful contacts with liberal colleagues in other mainline churches than I do with evangelical colleagues in my own denomination.

Wuthnow's insight is confirmed by the tremendous growth in parachurch groups, especially among evangelical Christians who have felt shut out by their (usually) liberal denominational structures. It is also confirmed by the ways in which power has shifted from formal denominational structures to affinity groups within many mainline churches. For example, pastors and members in my denomination pay far more attention to what is going on in the more liberal Covenant Network and the more evangelical Presbyterian Coalition—the two affinity groups that have formed out of the denomination's current debate over the ordination of homosexuals—than they do to what is coming out of Presbyterian national headquarters in Louisville. Both affinity groups are beginning to offer the sorts of services that, in the recent past, we have counted on denominational structures to provide—for example, networks in which pastors searching for new pastorates can find like-minded congregations, curricula, and youth conferences. Indeed, some in the evangelical group have called for the creation of "shadow structures" to serve the needs of evangelical congregations and ministers during the time (in their words) that the "denomination is being reclaimed" from what they perceive are its liberal distortions.

Loss of Brand Loyalty

Those most loyal to denominational institutions also feel this shift in the winds and are working hard to reassert "brand loyalty" in a time when the average church member feels very little loyalty to a particular church tradition. Have you asked the denominational background of people in your church's most recent new-member classes? If the mix is anything like what I experience, you'll find that they come to your congregation from many traditions—Protestant and Roman Catholic—or from having had no church experience at all. Perhaps, if they were Presbyterian in the last town where they worshiped, newcomers might give the Presbyterian church in their new town the first shot. However, if that congregation doesn't "feel" right or "meet our needs" (a gift with which American consumerism has lately graced the church), they will have no problem trying out the local United Methodist church, and the Episcopal parish, and on and on, until they have found the right "fit." There's nothing inherently wrong with church-shopping. It simply means that people are connecting with particular Christian communities for reasons other than the denominational logo on the sign out front.

A consumerist approach can have a negative impact on the church when congregations abandon their core beliefs to adopt a marketing strategy based on consumer values. The temptation to abandon core values is more likely to be evident in strategies that employ marketing categories to assess potential members' needs and then to custom-design ministries to meet those needs, regardless of whether those ministries embody the congregation's core values.

However, an awareness that we are entering a post-denominational era can encourage us to try to understand our own traditions at a deeper level so that we can separate the tradition's wheat from its chaff (and every tradition has its own fair share of chaff). It can also encourage us to reconsider the catholic tradition of the pre-Reformation church to rediscover theologically rich practices our various denominational families may have too cavalierly jettisoned during the Reformation. (Most Protestants can point to things our traditions have emphasized primarily because the practice is "*not* Roman Catholic"). This recovery has already begun. The Roman Catholic tradition rediscovered the importance of preaching during Vatican II, and many Protestant traditions have recently begun to call for more frequent celebrations of the Eucharist.

Every denominational tradition within the body of Christ holds some valuable gift, some particular charism, for the body as a whole (remember Paul's use of the analogy of the body in 1 Corinthians 12?). We are being invited by the Spirit to share our tradition's particular gifts generously with our brothers and sisters in the faith. We are also bidden to rejoice in the rediscovery of the gifts other traditions have preserved and now offer back to us. Each communion's life will be enriched as we rediscover the treasures other denominational families have preserved for us and begin to reincorporate them into our communities' lives.

Such a process of mutual sharing will free us from some of the more petty ways we have differentiated ourselves from one another and help us to affirm our commonality as joint heirs with Christ. It will also free us to appreciate what the particular traditions we embody in our denominational families have to offer the postmodern, post-Christian world in which we seek to be heralds of the good news of Jesus Christ. If we have eyes to see and ears to hear, we will develop a new postmodern catholicity that will define denominations as communities within the one holy catholic and apostolic church—communities that incarnate particular historically shaped practices and beliefs—rather than seeing them as warring, mutually exclusive sects.

A Radically Changed Landscape

No wonder we continually feel jostled and assaulted as we try to be helpful leaders of congregations. The landscape in which we seek to be faithful to our calling has radically shifted beneath our feet, and yet we have managed so far to act as if nothing had changed. This, in the final analysis, is probably too harsh an assessment of what we have done or failed to do as congregational leaders. It would be truer to say that it has been difficult for us to sense and respond to these changes in the cultural landscape because they have crept up on us so slowly and quietly. That nagging feeling that something is out of kilter has been accurate all along, but we haven't yet been able to face the changes head-on. It is as if we have been able to glimpse them only in the very periphery of our field of vision, through intimation of the Spirit. Having a fresh conceptual framework in which to set our hunches about this unfamiliar landscape, though, will help us to face this unanticipated situation head on and to learn how to be the Body of Christ in ways that will be both faithful to the gospel and responsive to this emerging cultural context.

CHAPTER 2

The Emerging Church

Once we catch on to the fact that the context in which we do ministry today is radically different from the prevailing context at the time some of us entered ministry a couple of decades ago, we begin to see why what we've "always done before" no longer works. It's as though we began our ministries playing a game of football in a football stadium, but when we came out of the locker room after halftime, the field had been rearranged for baseball. We wonder how these bases we keep tripping over got here, but we go on playing the second half as if we were still playing football. Just below consciousness, our kinesthetic sense tells us that the field has changed from a rectangle to a diamond; still, we wonder why we run out of bounds so quickly as we head toward the end of the field where home base is located.

A Shifting Paradigm

Slowly it dawns on us that our problem is that *the way we think about ministry is still rooted largely in a modernist paradigm more suited to the waning era of Christendom*—a conceptual framework for ministry that was still helpful through the 1970s for pastors in ministry at that time. Those who were clergy during the '70s and '80s were still, by and large, able to pull things off. In retrospect, many of us have realized that we were working with the last bits of social and ecclesial capital with which the twin concepts of modernity and Christendom provided the church. Those who entered ministry in the '90s and beyond have probably never enjoyed the sense of support that modernity and Christendom provided for so long.

For example, how often has your congregation invited the wider community to come hear a speaker or a seminar that you *know* should be of broad interest, only to see very few people from outside your own congregation show up for the event? The Christendom model assumed that most people of goodwill would be interested in what the church had to say about the issues of the day. A pastoral predecessor at a church I formerly served, I am told, learned that his Sunday evening sermons were being covered by a couple of metropolitan newspapers, because the community was eager to hear what a leading preacher in the community had to say about issues facing the city. Today, however, it would never enter the minds of an increasing number of people to listen to what the church has to say as they form their responses to the issues facing society.

It wasn't long ago that one could assume that most people who sat in new-member classes knew the basics of the biblical story. Pastors could assume that they understood something about the central doctrines of the faith, and knew what they were supposed to do when they came to worship and how they were expected to support the church with their money and energy. My guess is that many of the folk who join that class now are either trying out the Christian tradition for the first time or returning to congregational life for the first time since they were children. You quickly discover that you can't expect them to know much at all about the faith, either its beliefs or its practices. You suddenly realize that you're going to have to do a much more thorough job of formation for these folk than was required of the church 25 years ago. Merely teaching content *about* the faith, the reigning model of Christian education up until the last generation, isn't going to do the job. Rather, you will need to introduce people to the basic narrative of scripture, the spiritual disciplines of prayer and worship, and the shape of Christian living. Formation will need to replace education as our model of Christian nurture.

Despite the shifts we have experienced over the past couple of decades, our processes for enculturation and education worked well enough in our congregations until quite recently. We were getting enough new members who were already adequately formed in the Christian tradition to lead us to believe that old programs of Christian education were effective at helping people grow in faith. We could assume that everyone who came to worship knew the basic outline of the biblical story and understood what the congregation was doing as it gathered for worship. And while we may have sensed that the church wasn't quite running on all cylinders, the engine wasn't missing badly enough for us to pull off the side of the road and look under the hood.

Indeed, most of the books we read and the seminars we attend still assume that if you just "tweak" an existing program rooted in the old Christendom paradigm a bit, you can get your congregation hitting on all cylinders again. For example, if you adopt a new program for youth ministry or a different curriculum for your children's Christian education program, everything will be fine.

Our experience, though, is that the length of time elapsing between needed congregational tune-ups shortens with each successive look under the hood. Whatever new energy we see in the congregation's life as a result of these adjustments dissipates more rapidly with each attempt to change.

We Can't Wait

We know that our older models for instituting congregational renewal aren't working anymore. And we are beginning to see that one of the main reasons they aren't working is that they're rooted in a Christendom framework that no longer applies. But we don't yet understand enough about the emerging postmodern, post-Christian, and postdenominational era into which the Spirit is now leading the church to do anything more than guess at what might replace these older models.

Do you remember taking pictures with a Polaroid camera? (How quickly we have passed *that* image-making technology by!) As soon as you snapped a picture, the camera would eject what looked like a blank photograph. Slowly, over a couple of minutes, an image would emerge as the picture developed. First, only the slightest change in shading would be evident. Then the outlines of figures would become faintly visible. The picture continued to become incrementally clearer. Watching the emergence of what finally became a sharp and clear image was part of the fun of using a Polaroid camera.

In a similar way, we are only now beginning to take our first Polaroid snapshots of the new cultural context into which the church—along with the rest of society—is moving. The picture of that world is only beginning to emerge. We now can see only the barest outlines of its shape, contrast, and hue. If we are asked to guess how the picture is going to turn out, most of our guesses will probably be wrong. We just can't see the image clearly enough yet.

At the same time, our gut tells us that we don't have the luxury of waiting until the image is fully developed before we begin to make some radical changes in how we live out the gospel. If we wait until we are confident in our understanding of the newly emerging cultural context, American society will have moved beyond us. Americans will be living out their postmodern 21st-century lives while we offer them worship, education, and fellowship more suited to the mid-20th. If we wait until we are *sure* we know what to do, the church will have missed its best opportunity to proclaim the gospel in ways that postmodern Americans can hear.

The longer we speak in the cadences of modernity, the less interested postmoderns will be in making the effort to translate what we're saying. It will be as if the church and the culture were speaking two different languages, neither able to understand the other. It has always been the task of the church to translate the gospel into thought forms and patterns of speech that can be understood by ordinary people and that will draw them to God. The church needs to face squarely its renewed call to translate Christian speaking and living skillfully, not only preserving the core of the good news but also presenting that good news in ways intelligible to a postmodern, post-Christian culture.

How Do We Begin?

As Leo Tolstoy asked, what then should we do? How do we discover those new forms of church life that will faithfully re-present the gospel in a postmodern, post-Christian America? Try anything that pops into our minds? Encourage an ecclesial version of Mao's invitation to "let a thousand flowers bloom," and then sift through the experiments to see which ones work in this new context and which don't? Immerse ourselves again in the great tradition of the church to rediscover its core meaning, so that we can translate that core through new symbols and new patterns of living? Peruse the works of third-century theologians to learn how to be faithful in an alien culture?

I think the answer to *all* these questions is, at least in part, yes. When we know that what worked in the past no longer works, but we don't yet see what should replace our former practices, we need to step out intuitively and cautiously into the future until we can see more clearly.

Tony Robinson, one of the three pastors who offer a vision for hope for the church's future in the book *Good News in Exile,* talks about how he is intuitively adapting his ministry to our new situation: "I . . . began to sense that one of the best ways to bring about change is to go ahead and act on your best hunches, intuitions, and convictions, to live into the new reality that is breaking into the midst of the old, and not wait for permission or consensus to emerge."[1] The truth of the matter is that we don't really have much choice, unless we want to stick with a way of being the church that no longer makes much sense to younger Christians entering the church.

Developing Our Peripheral Vision

To stick with the image of "seeing" the future, if we can't see our way forward, maybe a different kind of sight is required, one that will enable us to move cautiously, but with hope, into the church's future.

Normally, as we move through life, we focus on what lies straight ahead. However, if we stop focusing on what lies directly in front of us, we will begin to notice objects in the periphery of our vision, objects that were there all along but that we did not notice because we were so focused on looking straight ahead. Sometimes, what we can see with our peripheral vision is the most important thing of all (for example, if you were on safari, it would be useful to notice that a lion was creeping up on you from the side!). Primarily using their peripheral vision is a native way of seeing for some albino people, but it will be a learned skill for most of us.

We are at a moment in the life of the church when what lies in our peripheral vision may well be far more important than what we see by looking straight ahead. Our intuitions, the nudges of the Spirit, and our hunches, as Robinson suggests, may provide a way forward out of the stuck place in which we now find ourselves. New images for the church's mission are beginning to appear as shimmering figures just at the edge of our peripheral vision. Often all we can discern is that something is jumping around. Occasionally, we are able to begin to sense its shape and the direction it's moving. But when we turn to look at the image head-on, it vanishes. Perhaps all we can do at this point in the church's history is to learn to pay attention to our peripheral vision. It may take a while for those shimmering images to shift into our direct line of sight, allowing us to describe them more clearly.

Examples of Developing Images

Here are a couple of examples of the kinds of changes I think we are beginning to glimpse in our peripheral vision.

We've all become aware of the degree to which television advertising has been affected by the editorial philosophy that guides the production of music videos shown on the cable channels MTV and VH-1. When you watch a music video, what you see on the screen cuts quickly from one image to another. No image lasts more than a few seconds. Shots are taken from all angles, and it doesn't really matter if the camera is held motionless or if the image jiggles a bit. If a live performance is shown, we see as many shots of the audience as of the performers. The camera zooms in or out or pans across the scene at a speed that leaves us a bit dizzy. Instead of having the sense of a single video with a linear plot, we have the sense that we're viewing a collage. The video invites the viewer to *experience* the video rather than to think about it. We find it easier to describe our holistic impression of the video (a right-brain ability) than to talk about its parts and their sequence from one to another (a left-brain ability). As a graffito I saw in the mid-'70s in Berkeley prophetically proclaimed, postmodern Americans tend to live by the adage "I *feel*, therefore I am."

Today's television ads for a whole range of products, but especially those targeted at a younger audience (for example, ads promoting "first-time-buyer" automobiles), are starting to look and sound like MTV videos. The music is loud, the video cuts quickly between shots, and the ads seek to impart a feeling more than to tell a story. Clearly a new way of telling a story is emerging in American culture.

Now, think for a minute about the implications of these changes for how we tell a story during worship. Will people raised on a steady diet of music videos want to sit through a 20-minute sermon, with a single "talking head" presenting a left-brain, linear exposition? Will a generation wed to images more than to words be moved to experience God's presence through responsive litanies? Would committing to a faster-paced, more image-driven liturgy be a means for preaching the gospel in a way that gen Xers and millennials can hear it, or would such changes sell out the Christian tradition?

These are the kinds of urgent questions we need to begin asking ourselves to help nudge intuitions from our peripheral vision into our direct line of sight. How will we communicate the gospel through worship in a culture more interested in *experiencing* the transcendent than in *learning about* the tension between God's transcendence and immanence? How will those of us for whom critical reflection is a foundational aspect of our theological journeys minister to people for whom experiencing is more important than thinking? And how will those who natively understand MTV's editing style minister to older members to whom music videos make no sense at all? We may not immediately come up with satisfying answers to these questions, but the sooner we begin to engage them directly, the sooner we will be able to discern the future shape of the church's mission. They are exactly the kinds of questions we must ask if we want to gain a clearer image of the emerging church.

Here's another example. Most of us conduct some sort of annual financial fund drive in our congregations, whether our boards simply set a budget and trust, in faith, that our members will give enough to fund it, or formally ask congregants for financial pledges. I would guess that most of our financial programs are based on the assumption that people already understand how the ministries of the church are funded. We assume they already know that their giving is the only (or at least the primary) source of income our board has for funding staff salaries, paying utility bills, and supporting the mission of the wider church. In the changing shape of our culture, however, that may be an erroneous assumption.

Jeffrey and Cynthia, a clergy couple who are friends of mine, were called to lead a new-church development in a booming area of a nearby city, where houses were going up as fast as developers could build them. Many younger families were attracted to the new congregation. The majority of them were coming into the church for the first time, often because they had young children for whom they wanted "some sort of moral education." My friends included me on their church newsletter's mailing list to keep me in touch with how their ministry was going.

Almost immediately, I began to notice articles by Jeffrey and Cynthia in which they listed all church expenses for the preceding month and patiently explained that the contributions of church members were the only source of money to pay those expenses. When I asked Cynthia about the articles, she said, "We quickly discovered that most of the folk worshiping with us thought that the money to pay our expenses just magically appeared. They assumed the national church, or the United Way, or *somebody* was paying the bills. They had no idea that churches rely on their own worshiping community to fund their ministry."

Soon afterward, I noticed articles about the financial needs of the church, gently explaining that a member's support of the church can't be modeled on the way one supports the Red Cross—a $50 gift at the end of the year. "That was the other cultural assumption they brought to church with them," Cynthia explained—"that if you made a gift to the church equivalent to the gift you made to all the other charities that sent you a fund-raising letter around Christmastime, then you'd done what you should."

All of us have struggled with the realization that we are losing to death a whole generation of longtime members who had developed a deep and faithful concept of the grace of liberality over the course of their lives and who paid annual pledges in the thousands of dollars. They are being replaced in our pews by newer, greener givers who assume that $100 a year is a generous gift in support of the congregation's ministry. New Christians, no matter their age, bring a different cultural assumption about how one financially supports the church than do longer-term church members. Like Jeffrey and Cynthia, all of us are going to have to be far more intentional in forming faithful givers. It's not that our new members will resist such formation; rather, they have never been told what the church means by financial stewardship, and they have never seen faithful stewardship in action. During our fall budget drive, we often ask a few of our more faithful givers to talk about what stewardship means to them and how they decide what proportion of their resources to commit to the church's mission. We've found that these personal testimonies, especially when told by people who can express what they feel as well as what they think about church giving, have had a profound impact on developing an understanding of stewardship among our newer members.

A Name for What We See

I find it helpful to name what is beginning to shimmer in our collective peripheral field of vision as the "emerging church." A new way of "doing" and "being" the mission of God in a postmodern, post-Christian culture, the emerging church often reveals itself in liminal experiences—bubbling up slowly from the ground of our awareness, showing itself just beyond the threshold of our ability to see it clearly. Its outlines are faint. We can't yet discern the exact shape it will take. It's far too early to describe the developing image accurately. But we all have had experiences like the ones I've just described—experiences that hint at where we should look for the birth of this new way of being church. My guess is that within 50 years, we'll all be able to discern its shape far more clearly. But that doesn't mean we don't have the resources to *begin* that discernment right now.

The outline of the emerging church will become clearer over time through a bottom-up rather than a top-down process. It won't be handed down to congregations from on high by academic theologians who don't engage daily in the messy experience of trying to build Christian community in a changing cultural context. Rather, any consensus will emerge only as thousands of pastors, lay leaders, and congregations begin to experiment. They will begin to work with their best hunches. They will talk with other Christians about what they're learning. Together, they will begin to describe where the Spirit is leading the church.

The process through which the emerging church will make itself known will necessarily be messy; it may occasionally lead to conflict. However, if our deepest desire is to be faithful to God through our congregational life, we can begin to experiment, follow hunches, and trust that the Spirit will help us discern the most faithful forms of emerging church life. Trying to figure out the shape of the emerging church is not a luxury for those of us who lead Christian communities. The new cultural context demands it.

If we continue to rely upon forms of church life developed for a modernist context and an Enlightenment approach to the world, young Christians and seekers of all ages whose worldview is shaped by neither of those influences will increasingly find our congregations less-than-faithful expressions of God's mission in the world. The current pressure to make changes in particular areas of church life—for example, to provide "more contemporary" worship services or flatter, less formal governance structures—will, over time, reveal itself as a demand for a way of "being church" wholly formed by postmodern, post-Enlightenment perspectives. In fact, the emerging church is already making itself known. Denominationally distinctive liturgies are already giving way to a wide variety of worship styles. Rethinking what it means to be involved in mission is another sign of the emerging church. Do we do mission in far-off lands, or close to home? Is it *our* mission or *God's* mission to which we are invited? (The Gospel and Our Culture Network—a group of North American thinkers inspired by British missiologist Lesslie Newbigin[2]—insists that it is the latter.)

But how can we know whether what we glimpse in our peripheral vision is, in fact, that emerging church toward which the Spirit draws us? Our current experimentation can lead either to more faithful or less faithful forms of church life for the future. Our hunches will not always be right, or Spirit-filled. Just as the author of 1 John reminds us to "test the spirits to see whether they are from God" (1 John 4:1), so must we test over time whether our experiments are faithful to God, and whether they produce the fruits of the Spirit in the dawning postmodern era. In a word, we are called to practice *discernment.* Not every idea we have about changing the forms of church life to adapt to a postmodern context will be a winner. Not all of them will be "from God." The task before us is one of corporate spiritual discernment.

Guidelines for Discernment

Here are four guidelines for the process of discernment that I suggest from what I have learned about it from my own ministry setting.

*First, pray for the guidance of the Holy Spirit as you begin
the process of discernment, and assume that you will be
granted that gift.*

Many of us mainline Christians are a bit leery about praying
for the gift of guidance from the Spirit. We are far more comfortable with the first two persons of the Trinity than we are
with the third. And yet, even stipulating our unease with
language about the Spirit, we are now being called to a task
of discernment for which the gift of the Spirit is an essential
tool. We will not have the wisdom on our own to know which
of our experiments and hunches will be most faithful and
most useful for the mission of God in this new era. What we
need is Holy Wisdom, the leadership of the Holy Spirit, to
lead us toward the more faithful options before us. We will
need to learn to trust that the Spirit is eager to lead us through
this discernment process. Indeed, much of the blame for the
"dryness" in mainline congregational life today can be at-
tributed to the ways we shut ourselves off from the Spirit's
energy and leadership. When Jesus promised his disciples
that the Spirit would guide them "into all truth" (John 16:13),
they were facing a situation similar to our own. The context
in which they sought to follow Jesus was about to change
radically with his death and resurrection. No longer could
they rely on his leadership to show them the way; now they
would have to find it on their own. The Spirit, Jesus assured
them, would help them discover new ways to follow him
faithfully on the other side of resurrection. We now find ourselves at a similar moment of change in context; and, like the
Twelve, we can be confident that the Spirit will lead us to
discover new ways to follow our Savior faithfully in *this* new
context for ministry.

*Second, understand that whatever new shape of
congregational life we discover through discernment, it
must remain consistent with the tradition of which we are
heirs, and especially with the ministry, death, and
resurrection of Jesus Christ.*

If we are to continue to call ourselves Christian, then—no matter what forms our congregational life may take—what those forms contain must be that same *kerygma* (core of the gospel) to which the Spirit has always led the church to give witness. We can get so caught up in the efficacy of new forms of church life that we lose sight of whether they tell the central story of God's love for humanity, revealed finally in Jesus as the Christ. We can't, for example, be satisfied with a new style of worship that attracts many new people if that worship is not focused on the praise of God in Christ through the power of the Holy Spirit. Success does not always equal faithfulness. Many worship styles entertain the congregation but fail to proclaim the *kerygma* fully. Certainly, in the years ahead as in the past, the Spirit will continue to help us gain new insights into the timeless truth God revealed in Jesus Christ.

Some of our intuitions will lead us to suggest changes that are readily seen to be consistent with the Christian tradition as we have received it. Other changes we suggest in our attempt to be faithful to our new context for ministry will be perceived as radically departing from that tradition. Any proposal that is perceived as such a departure from the tradition will bear a greater burden of proof before the church decides that the proposal is, in fact, "of God." Those who propose the change will need to show how it is consistent with the deeper layers of the Christian tradition, even though on the surface it may appear radically different. That doesn't mean a radically new direction *can't* be where the Spirit is leading us, just that the warrant for its faithfulness will be greater for those suggesting it. For example, no matter where you stand on the issue, the proposal to ordain people who are in same-sex covenantal relationships requires a clearer warrant of faithfulness to the tradition from those who support it *because* it asks the church to adopt a radically different understanding of the moral status of same-sex relationships than it has proclaimed for the past 2,000 years. This is not just a matter of making a slight adjustment in the trajectory of the church's tradition about sexual morality; it is a major reinterpretation of that tradition. Those among us who believe we are following the Spirit's leading in this particular discernment process will need to be ready to tell how we understand the change to be consistent with the great tradition of the church.

> *Third, find colleagues—both clergy and lay—who are also seeking to be open to the leading of the Spirit in this enterprise, and compare notes with them.*

The process of discerning the outlines of the emerging church cannot be a solitary pursuit. We will need one another for both encouragement and mutual critique. Talking with colleagues who also are seeking to pay attention to *their* fields of peripheral vision not only serves to confirm our intuitions but also helps everyone involved in the conversation to see more clearly. As we are being healed from the cataracts of modernity, we will often mistake what we see, especially as those images *first* begin to emerge in our peripheral vision. Colleagues who are paying attention as we are can help us discern whether it is really trees we see, or people (see Mark 8:24). We can have more confidence in our hunches and our experiments in ministry when they are congruent with the intuitions of people whom we trust also to be open to the leading of the Spirit. Conversely, we need to think again about those guesses we make when colleagues we trust tell us they don't think our most recent hunch will take us in the direction the Spirit is calling the church to go.

> *Fourth, as you begin to employ your best guesses, watch to see if they produce good fruit of the Spirit.*

If you change the structure or the "feel" of your liturgy in a way that you think will be more faithful in the emerging church, for example, listen for the feedback you receive. Do people tell you the changes bring them more fully into the presence of God or better enable them to express their thanks and praise to God? Or if you are seeking to lead your congregation in the practice of group discernment, are you hearing people say that the process helps them listen more carefully to God's leadership in the decision you are making together? Especially because we are feeling our way into the emerging church, our intuitions about where the Spirit is leading us may be fully known only in hindsight. All along the way of discernment—at its beginning and at its end— we will need to ask whether what we propose bears the "fruit of the Spirit": love, joy, peace, patience, kindness, generosity, faithfulness, gentleness, and self-control (Gal. 5:22).

Discerning the shape of the emerging church will be an inexact process, especially for those of us who still have one foot firmly planted back in the old modernist and Christendom paradigm and are only beginning to understand the impact of the new postmodern and post-Christian context for ministry. Because that process will often be confusing, we need the Holy Spirit to lead us through it. If we could rely *only* on our own bumbling efforts at discerning the shape of the emerging church, we would be in trouble. As a friend once described the way a new pastor is called to lead a congregation, "It's so crazy, you *have* to believe the Holy Spirit is in charge; or you'd go nuts!" In a similar way, we would be tempted to despair in our attempts to discover the emerging church, were we not confident that the Spirit is at work in and through us.

Sharing My Own Intuitions

Davis Community Church of Davis, California, the congregation of which I was a co-pastor for more than 15 years, was wonderfully open to adopting these four guidelines in its own attempt to be open to new ways of being the church. Both its leadership and the congregation as a whole were willing to experiment and play out our corporately discerned best hunches. Along with those of us in leadership, the church members consistently prayed for the guidance of the Holy Spirit as, together, we made our "best guesses" about the shape of the emerging church.

What follows in the next several chapters is a reflection on the process of discernment we shared as pastors and congregation at the Davis church. I will tell you some of what we learned about the emerging church in four important areas of congregational life: worship, formation, mission, and governance. I will share our intuitions about the shape of the emerging church—not to suggest that we figured everything out (because we didn't—not by a long shot!), but to encourage you in your own process of experimentation and discernment. In reading this book, you become a colleague in this process of discernment in the body of Christ, open to the leadership of the Spirit in your own setting for ministry as you experiment and try out your best hunches. I hope our fledgling attempts to discern the shape of the emerging church will encourage you to begin your own discernment process and to share what you learn with others near you who peer longingly in the same direction as you.

CHAPTER 3

Worship in the Emerging Church

Corporate worship is at the heart of the Christian community. Everything of importance to the life of the emerging church is rooted in this central act in which the community offers its praise to God:

- its commitment to form people into followers of Christ,
- its desire to share with the world the good news it has received, and
- its call to show forth a distinctive form of community life in its polity.

Corporate worship is also the primary point of entry into the Christian community for people new to the faith.

Although a variety of patterns for worship scheduling are beginning to emerge in American churches, the Sunday morning worship service is still the primary focal point for congregational life. At no other time in the week are so many members of a particular Christian community gathered in one place to experience what it means to be a member of the body of Christ. What we do during worship will shape how worshipers experience themselves as members of that body of Christ through the remainder of the week. Because so many of the people coming to our services for the first time have little or no background in, or understanding of, the nature of worship, we need to think carefully about how we plan and lead our liturgies.

Worship is the heart of the body that circulates the Spirit's life-giving energy into the rest of the church's life. A church whose engagement in mission is not rooted in its worship life will soon discover its most dedicated members burned out and its mission waning. A congregation whose educational ministry is not fed by its worship life will soon wake up to realize that its adult-education program has become focused on passing on information *about* the faith rather than on forming people *in* the faith. A community whose church governance is not energized by its worship life will find its church board behaving more like a secular nonprofit organization's board of directors than a body called together to discern the will of God for a local Christian community. Worship shapes the faith and the faithfulness not only of the individual worshiper but also of the community as a whole.

Worship is the primary classroom in which we have the opportunity to teach the faith. Because we typically see far more of our members in worship than in Christian education classes, the Sunday morning worship service is the main setting in which we can pass on the great tradition of the church. This fact doesn't mean that all our sermons need to be teaching sermons, though we probably ought to think of the sermon as a teaching moment more often than we do. Rather, it means that we ought always to think *pedagogically* about what we are doing in worship. We can teach through the hymns and songs we choose. We can teach by carefully weaving the formative images of the tradition into our prayers and responses. We can teach by designing our liturgies in a "call and response" format that by its very shape helps worshipers experience God's call to us in worship and elicit our response to that call.

Worship is the setting in which worshipers experience being a people shaped by the biblical narrative. Postmoderns come to us shaped by any *number* of narratives: the narrative of success, for example, or the narrative that tells us, "The one who dies with the most toys wins." Worship is where we experience God's invitation to live in a world very different from the one offered by the cacophony of narratives that shape the various lifestyle niches of the wider culture today. It provides the context in which new worshipers can learn that we are the *ecclesia,* a community called out from the world. Stanley Hauerwas reminds us that it's presumptuous to think we are not shaped by a narrative external to ourselves. Rather, he would say, individuals and communities like the church have the option only of deciding *which* narrative will shape our lives. It has been a long time since the church could count on the broader culture to send it people already half-formed in a Christian worldview. The once-heralded three-legged stool of Christian formation that operated for much of America's history—church, home, and school—now teeters, by and large, on one leg: the church. Worship is our primary opportunity to offer people another perspective on the world, another way to imagine life: a way of life shaped by the life, ministry, death, and resurrection of the One we call the Christ. One hour a week may not be much to work with, but we have to make the best use of what people will, at least in the beginning, give us.

Worship is also the studio in which we learn the art of being Christian. More and more of the people who are coming into our churches today either have never been churchgoers before or haven't been in worship since they were first able at age 13 or so to resist their parents' demand that they attend. Because postmodern people are more interested in their experience of, rather than their understanding of, worship, we need to think about what experience we are providing them in our liturgies.

In part, new worshipers' need to "experience" means that we must consider some practical issues. These new worshipers are trying to make sense of the hymnal. (In what other book do you read one line of text and then skip down three lines before reading the next line of text?) They are nervously looking around to see when to stand, when to sit, and whether they're supposed to put something in that plate when it comes down the pew. More important, they don't know what it means to pray. (In my last parish, even though it exasperated some of our longtime members, we printed the text of the Lord's Prayer in our bulletin every Sunday. We assumed that at least *one* person in each service wouldn't have the slightest idea what to say at that moment if we didn't print the words.)

We need to realize that the new people in our sanctuaries probably aren't even sure what the purpose of worship is, where God "is," how they are supposed to experience God's presence or to present themselves to God. Therefore, we are called to engage in basic Christian formation with most of the people who enter our worship spaces today. Formation is more like an apprenticeship in the arts than it is a formal course of instruction. It is about practice and attitude as much as it is about content. People will learn what it means to be Christian by participating in the worshiping community, by learning its distinctive language, and by incorporating its distinctive rhythms into their lives. In 12-step communities, such an apprenticeship is referred to through the use of the term "acting as if." By "acting as if" they are sober, AA members will over time learn to be sober. Similarly, by "acting as if" they are Christians by participating in the formative actions of worship, people new to the faith will one day wake to discover that they have become followers of Jesus Christ.

Worship provides an experience of the body of Christ through which we discover that we are not isolated and independent creatures. Contrary to everything the Enlightenment's emphasis on individualism has told us, we are neither separate from one another nor self-determined, but we belong to a community called into being in Christ. The experience of communal worship develops in us an awareness that we belong first to God and then to one another as sisters and brothers in Christ. By regularly experiencing ourselves to be part of this body of Christ, we are given both the vision and the courage to resist the hyperindividualism of our age. And we are given the vision and courage to resist modernity's overweening faith in progress that tempts us to assume that our present generation sees things much more clearly than any preceding one. As we immerse ourselves in the great liturgical tradition of the church, we become more deeply connected with the saints of all centuries. This connection helps us be more open to letting the time-tested wisdom of that tradition critique and correct our modernist impulses.

Most foundationally, though, worship is the holy of holies, wherein we encounter the living God. How sad it is that we all have had far too many experiences of leaving a mainline worship service and asking ourselves, "Where was God in all of that?" We may have heard a well-prepared and excellently delivered sermon but heard little of the gospel. We may have listened to a fine pipe organ and sung some of our favorite hymns or praise songs but departed from worship with our hearts strangely cooled. Worship in mainline churches has tended to become flattened over the past half-century. It is a wonderful experience of human community in the horizontal dimension. We know who is in need of prayer and the opportunities for service and mission in the week ahead, and we have had a warm experience of being with people we genuinely like. And yet the transcendent dimension of worship is often missing. Unless we help people experience God's presence or create a setting in which they are able truly to offer thanks and praise to God, then it makes no difference how finely we craft our sermons or how carefully we select our anthems. Postmodern people are hungry to experience the divine. They're not particularly interested in how thoughtful a preacher you are. They're not even especially concerned about whether your church uses an organ or a guitar as its primary musical instrument. They care far more about encountering the living God in your liturgy.

Worship as Christian Immersion

In Davis, California, the community in which I last served, the public schools offer Spanish immersion school for children in grades K-6. The program is designed primarily for children whose native language is English. From the first day they enter the classroom, their teachers speak to them only in Spanish, even in the kindergarten classes. It is a frustrating struggle for the first several weeks, but eventually the children begin to respond in Spanish as well. Later they will grasp the syntax and grammar of the Spanish language in a more formal sense, but the immersion model enables them to learn the language "from the inside out." They don't have to think in English first, and then translate into Spanish. They learn to think as well as speak in their new language. They have a good chance of becoming truly bilingual.

Theirs is a very different experience from that of students who take Spanish as a separate subject in an otherwise English-based curriculum. These nonimmersion students may also have a teacher who speaks to them only in Spanish for that one period a day, but the way they imagine and think about the world will still be shaped by English grammar and syntax. English will, far and away, remain their primary language.

We need to begin to think of worship as Christian immersion, because most of the new worshipers coming into our worship spaces do not know the grammar and syntax of the Christian tradition. They may have seen on rare occasions a televised worship service, or heard someone pray at a public gathering (a rarer experience these days). Their exposure to the language and imagery of the Christian tradition is so slight, however, that we can pretty safely assume that most of what we say in our liturgies will sound to them like a foreign language. Our temptation will be to explain the peculiar language of the Christian faith to them in terms with which they are more familiar—particularly in the language of psychology or sociology.

But by doing so, we have bought into the modernist assumption that we can successfully translate the particular language and grammar of the Christian tradition into a universal language—an assumption increasingly challenged by postmodern theorists. As is often the case, something is lost in the act of translation—in this case, something very precious. We ought to invite newcomers to stick with us long enough to glimpse the particular world into which our distinctive Christian language and images invite them. Even our longer-time members tend to be more conversant in the language of psychology and sociology than they are in the language of scripture. They are not able to see the world in a singularly Christian way because we have not given them the necessary tools. We have not helped them develop a native Christian vocabulary with which to speak of the things of the world.

We need, in the words of the author of the book of Revelation to the church at Ephesus, to return to the "love you had at first." If we are to practice worship as Christian immersion, we need to design our liturgies so that they are soaked, through and through, in the language of scripture. We need to tell those stories, over and over again, that will help our members grasp "from the inside out" the deep meaning of terms like sin and grace, freedom and service. We need to develop the language of faith as their first language, to enable them to think and dream in it.

Worship as Encounter with God

Postmodern people are hungry for an experience of the transcendent. But how many of our services of worship offer an experience of awe, of the majesty and presence of the Creator of the universe? I'm not talking about manufactured feelings or manipulated emotions, but about the ways we think through our liturgy to make sure that spaces are left in which the Almighty can be sensed and felt.

Every congregation will create the space for this encounter with God differently. Each congregation needs to think about the rhythm of its own liturgy, the architectural context for its worship, its choice of music, its use of visual and performing arts, and the language that shapes its liturgy. It needs to think about them with this question in mind: "How does our liturgy provide opportunities for the presence of the living God to break into our worship?"

It can be as simple a matter as introducing moments of silence into the service, in which worshipers are intentionally invited to listen for God's word to them. Tony Campolo, a Baptist educator who has done much to bridge the chasm between mainliners and evangelicals in America in recent years, has described our prayer life (and, by extension, our worship) as a strange long-distance call. It's as if we call a long-lost friend, talk nonstop for an hour about how things are with us, and then hang up. When our spouse asks us what our friend had to say, our only possible response is "Huh?"

Mainline churches tend to have a bad case of verbal diarrhea: we fill the hour of worship with words heaped upon words. We *tell* God everything about us, but we rarely incorporate space in our worship to listen for a word *from* God, even though we may open our reading of scripture with such a formula as "Listen to the Word of God." We are much better at talking than at listening. Sometimes one gets the sense that we're so afraid of what God might have to say to us that we fill the service completely with words to avoid giving the Almighty space to get a word in edgewise.

Several years ago, we began to include a moment for silent reflection after each of the scripture readings and the sermon. We didn't allow much time for silence—only about 30 seconds after each reading and about a minute after the sermon. But even that little silence was enough to make good Presbyterians crawl out of their skin with anxiety. Over time, however, these times of silence became the most important moments in worship for many parishioners.

"I feel as though I can let God's word sink into my bones," one congregant said.

"I often get my deepest insights into God's call to me during those silences," said another.

"I am so glad simply to have the opportunity to just sit in silence and experience the presence of God in the midst of the community."

Worship as Experience

Postmodern seekers are not interested in a "from the neck up" style of worship that may once have appealed to modern Christians. They are looking for a much more holistic worship experience that engages all the senses and appeals to the right brain more than to the left. I don't mean to say that every Presbyterian or Methodist church ought to go out and buy incense, but congregations *are* going to need to think about how they can involve the whole person in worship. My own Reformed tradition is notoriously asensual in its worship. At best, we engage two of our senses: primarily hearing and a bit of sight. That's just not going to cut it, for younger worshipers especially. Oral/aural worship services will put them to sleep even faster than such services did their grandparents. If we don't engage more than two of their senses, they'll go to a church that does, however rich or poor the theology mediated through that experience may be.

The liturgical renewal movement introduced color into the sanctuaries of previously nonliturgical mainline churches. Now there are few mainline churches that don't offer visual stimulation in worship at least through the use of stoles and paraments, or banners. But aren't there other ways we make use of color and texture and movement to draw a visually focused MTV generation deeper into the experience of worship? Wouldn't experimenting with greater use of the visual or performing arts in worship make it more likely that postmodern seekers will actually encounter God in our services?

Another change in worship that can reach out to postmoderns is embodied prayer. An important critique younger Christians have of the way the modern church practices its faith is that older Christians are not in touch with their bodies as they worship. The body/mind or body/soul dichotomy that marked most modernist thought is giving way to a more holistic understanding of what it means to be human. Postmoderns don't want to think *or* feel; they want to think/feel/be. And they want to think/feel/be in the presence of God. "Why just worship God with your mind," they ask, "when we are asked to give our whole selves to God?" They are interested in exploring how our bodily postures and movements can become, in and of themselves, forms of prayer. We mainline Christians tend to be uncomfortable with those who want to turn their hands upward as a sign of their willingness to receive God's blessing in prayer, or who want to kneel before the divine. But these kinesthetic forms of devotion can be very important to a postmodern who wants to give the whole self to God. Can we let go of our mainline anxieties about bodily posture and movement in worship? And can we allow people to embody their devotion in a variety of ways in corporate worship without "requiring" any particular norms about movement? I remember a professor at the Episcopal seminary at which I occasionally worshiped during my own seminary years, who had already intuited something about the dawning postmodern era in the 1970s. If everyone else knelt for prayer, he would stand; but if everyone else stood, he would kneel. He believed it was critical that people be given permission to express their piety in a variety of ways within a single Christian community. He set an example for us all.

Two embodied modes of worship became an important part of our congregation's life over the past few years. We began to receive communion by intinction, inviting people to dip a piece of communion bread into the chalice and take both elements at the same time. We also began to offer monthly rituals of wholeness as part of our regular Sunday morning worship.

Eucharistic Piety as Embodied Prayer

For many years, Davis Community Church followed the typical low-church pattern of quarterly communion, with the elements received in what I sometimes kiddingly refer to as "shot glasses and bread cubes." Several years before I arrived, the session (church governing board) had increased the frequency of communion to once a month, but the elders were still passing trays of individual cups and bread cubes along the rows of worshipers.

About 10 years ago, however, our board decided to begin alternating the way in which we administer the sacrament. Not quite ready to make the leap to drinking from a common cup, we began serving communion by intinction at one of our two Sunday morning services, and with cups and trays at the other, alternating intinction between the first and the second services from one month to the next. We invited people to leave their pews and to go to one of four stations around the sanctuary.

At about this same time, we were running out of space in the sanctuary and began planning for a third worship service. Not wanting to schedule an hour in which we offered worship and Christian education concurrently, we decided instead to hold two worship services simultaneously at 11 A.M. The new worship service, "Worship in the Round," included a weekly celebration of communion (still a rarity in Presbyterian circles) by intinction.

Both the change to communion by intinction and the opportunity for weekly communion immediately elicited positive responses from worshipers. One young woman talked about the joy of watching people's faces as they came forward to receive the elements, naming it "an experience of being part of a community, of being a member of the body of Christ." Another member spoke to me of the meaning he derived from the simple fact of getting up out of the pew and walking down the center aisle to commune, describing it as a form of walking meditation, much like walking a labyrinth. People who were drawn to the rhythm of weekly Eucharist talked about how much it meant to them for us to quit talking about the faith so much and simply to experience it. They all focused on the new opportunities we were giving them to engage the body in prayer—in walking, in eating, and in honoring others by honoring their bodily presence in community. Postmodern people crave the nonverbal and immediate experience of God's presence that the more embodied experience of the sacrament provided.

I knew we had uncovered a deep need when one of our elders, a former Southern Baptist recently turned Presbyterian, asked to see me for just a few minutes to talk about a proposal he wanted to bring to our church board. "I have never been so moved by communion as I have been since we began receiving it by intinction," he began. "There's just something about getting up out of your seat and moving forward to look a brother or sister in the eye when they say, 'The body of Christ, given for you.' Something happens in that exchange. I feel Christ's presence in a way I just don't experience it when someone passes the elements down the pew to me."

The board decided to adopt his suggestion that we serve the sacrament by intinction at *all* of our services on Communion Sundays. This elder wanted as many people as possible to have the more embodied experience of the sacrament he now enjoyed, and he clearly expected that most worshipers would also desire that more fully embodied experience of God's grace. That's a long way for a former Southern Baptist to move!

Services of Wholeness as Embodied Prayer

Another embodied form for worship has been recovered in recent years in mainline Protestant traditions that didn't previously have it—the service of wholeness and healing. The current Presbyterian *Book of Common Worship*, for example, contains several liturgies for services of wholeness for use with individuals and for corporate worship. This is a startling departure from the Reformed tradition's past queasiness about embodied forms of worship, as well as from its former rejection of a practice it considered "too Roman."

We mainline pastors make a connection between prayer and healing when we pray for the health of those who are ill or undergoing surgery, but we tend not to be so comfortable with considering the power of prayer to *effect* healing. We want to leave the actual healing in the hands of practitioners of the medical and psychological sciences. We don't want people to think we're like those televangelists who shout "Come out!" to demons, and throw back their wailing supplicant into the waiting arms of fellow congregants.

But in rightly wanting to avoid such excesses, we have not always heeded the clear call of scripture, "Are any among you sick? They should call for the elders of the church and have them pray over them, anointing them with oil in the name of the Lord" (James 5:14).

Recent double-blind studies on "distance healing" and the effectiveness of prayer as a partner to medical treatment of illness have shown even us "doubting Thomas" children of the Enlightenment that prayer does, in fact, have the power to heal. Especially when healing is understood holistically and not necessarily as the cure of a particular disease, prayers for healing and services for wholeness can play an important role in the care of souls we practice within our congregations.

Congregations will need to find the best ways to incorporate prayers for healing into their own services. No one pattern will fit every Christian community. Those in our congregations steeped in the modernist paradigm may be a bit leery at first and need interpretation of what we intend (and don't intend) as we begin offering services of wholeness. Postmoderns, however, will almost literally jump at the chance to have someone lay hands on them and pray over them. They natively understand the power of touch to heal and will appreciate this opportunity to give bodily expression to their faith.

We chose to institute monthly rituals of wholeness as part of our regular Sunday morning worship, rather than to offer a separate service of wholeness at a time other than Sunday morning. We did it this way because we wanted the congregation to understand that the laying on of hands and prayers for healing are consistent with and an extension of the more familiar means of grace they regularly experience in Sunday worship.

On those Sundays our prayers of confession focused on sin in terms of our dis-ease with God's desires for us and the lack of health and wholeness in us that comes from failing to follow in God's ways. The pastoral prayer might include petitions for recovery from all that makes us sick—in body, mind, and spirit. As the service ended, individuals were invited to come forward and to kneel at the front of the church.

A combination of clergy and laity were present to pray for those who came forward. We offered the simple prayer, "Jane, may God deliver you from all evil, preserve you in all goodness, release you from all suffering, and restore you to wholeness and health. Amen." If the person made a specific request for healing, we would incorporate that petition into our prayer. The laying on of hands during this simple prayer was a sign both of the transmission of God's healing love into their bodies and their lives and of the extension of God's blessing to them.

Embodying the Faith in Leadership

I remember the story once told me about a woman who visited a public-school classroom on Martin Luther King, Jr.'s birthday. She was asked to speak to the class about racial justice and inclusiveness. As she entered the classroom, however, she noticed that the teacher had pictures of great Americans plastered along the tops of the walls around the classroom—and that all of the pictures were of Euro-American males. "Right then and there," she later recounted, "I knew that whatever I said wasn't going to make that much of a difference. What was being shown to those children every day through those pictures was going to shape them far more powerfully than anything I had to say."

We forget how powerfully we demonstrate the congregation's self-understanding by our choices of whom to invite into positions of public leadership in its life, and especially in its worship services. This truth grows in importance as our congregations are made up more and more of gen X and younger Christians. They are generally distrustful of hierarchy and suspicious of anyone (even a preacher) who gets up and portrays herself to be a sole authority figure. Postmoderns believe that knowledge is held corporately in the community rather than in any single individual. They also have grown up in a world where equality between men and women has been preached for as long as they can remember. They accept diversity in the culture as a matter of course, having grown up in a diverse school system.

They are generations ripe for a radical recovery of the Protestant principle of the "priesthood of all believers." They aren't necessarily pressing for us to drop our commitment to an educated clergy. They are not as willing as Christians before them were, however, to accept a pastor's authority unquestioningly or to accept the clergy's interpretation of scripture without an opportunity for other voices and points of view to be heard and considered by the community.

The Davis congregation has had a male-female clergy team since the late 1970s. It's hard (though certainly not outside the realm of the Spirit's leading) to imagine that this congregation would ever be happy again with all male pastors (or all female, for that matter). They appreciate the complementarity of approaches to ministry and life that having both a male and a female pastor brings to the church's experience of community.

But being a male-female pastoral team didn't mean that Mary Lynn (my colleague) and I were never tempted to manipulate the authority granted to pastors. Perhaps the only change was that parishioners projected their emotions onto both pastors as their "cosmic mommy *and* daddy." Nonetheless, having two pastors instead of one led the congregation to wrestle with questions like "Where does the buck stop?" That wrestling helped us to give both better theological answers ("The buck stops with God") and better polity answers ("In our system, the buck stops with the session) to that question. In worship, it ensured that the congregation heard consistently from more than one voice in its preaching, thus resisting the "sole authority" model of pastoral leadership. The co-pastor model, thoughtfully implemented, has much to offer the church (enough so that I wish our polities would give broader permission for co-pastor teams to form). In particular, it can help churches begin to move from hierarchical structures toward structures in which power is shared more broadly. When two people at least are asked to share authority (even if initially that is still at the top of a pyramid power structure), a congregation's imagination can be stimulated to begin to wonder in faith about how broadly authority can be shared. It can help them dream of new ways to give practical form to our belief in the priesthood of all believers.

Leveling the playing field between clergy, then, is not nearly enough. Leadership in the congregation needs to be widely shared with lay leaders throughout the life of the church if we are to witness effectively to the priesthood of all believers. Worship is one of the most regular settings in which we give public witness about the kinds of people who exercise leadership in the life of the congregation. For this reason, we had a variety of laity lead worship along with the pastors every Sunday morning as a sign that the corporate worship of God is, indeed, a "liturgy," a work of the people. To give the fullest possible witness to our belief, we trained and included all kinds of people as lay worship leaders: men and women, youth and seniors and all ages in between, people of different races, gay people and straight. Having a wide variety of worship leaders was one of the ways we gave witness to our commitment to be an inclusive community of people seeking to follow in the way of Christ and to practice the priesthood of all believers. What we do speaks far more powerfully than what we say.

These surely are not all the ways we can change our thinking about liturgical design and leadership. But they are important examples of an emerging understanding about what it means to be a worshiping community in the postmodern era. Each of us is called to pray and think deeply about worship in our own settings for ministry and to begin to experiment with ways to make it both more transparent to the presence of the transcendent God and more accessible for the new generations of seekers after Christ who are entering our sanctuary doors.

Chapter 4

Christian Formation: Starting from Scratch

At the beginning of my ordained ministry in the late '70s, I could safely assume that almost everyone who came through the congregation's new-member class already more or less understood what Christianity was "all about." I could trust that they knew the broad sweep of the biblical story and that they understood what we were doing when we gathered as a community for worship or prayer. I could assume that they saw the world through Christian lenses (though their prescription for those lenses might have been slightly out of date).

I could get away with making these assumptions because the civil religion of America was still rooted deeply enough in a worldview formed largely by the biblical narrative. By osmosis if nothing else, this civil religion seeped into most Americans, still shaping them as late as the 1970s into something like low-church Protestants. We were beginning to see in our pews a sprinkling of folk who knew little about the story of Jesus, but they were the exceptions.

Needless to say, such knowledge can no longer be taken for granted. If you want proof of the change in what we can safely assume, go ask the English teachers at your local high school how many of their students pick up on the biblical allusions peppered throughout the classics of American literature. To a teacher, they will say, "Basically, none of them." Or ask how long it's been since the students in any of your local public schools sang Christmas carols as part of their celebration leading up to what is now called "winter break" rather than Christmas break. If any echoes of a Christian worldview reverberate faintly in American civic religion to-day, they are found in such generalized abstractions from that worldview as "Be nice, be fair, and be tolerant."

In the California congregations I served (and I would guess this would be true no matter where in the country you live), the culture is now very different. The vast majority of people coming into our churches have never been church-goers. Either that or they are coming back to the church (in our case for the past 10 years, at the average age of 36) for the first time in years and years. Often it is the birth of a child and the desire for that child to receive some sort of moral education that brings newcomers through our doors.

Many of them are what church literature now commonly calls "seekers," people who, before attending your church, may have described themselves as "spiritual, but not reli-gious." While we may either shake our heads sadly or poke mild fun at such a self-designation, it points toward some-thing crucially important for the emerging church. A deep spiritual hunger prevails in America today among people who long for meaning and depth in their lives. Those of us who are Christian trust that the meaning and depth for which they seek has been revealed in Jesus.

A growing longing for the transcendent is also evident among postmoderns. They desperately hope that life has more to offer than what they find on the surface, and they have a hunch that the church might be a place to find that "something more." While they come into our churches seek-ing an immanent experience of community, they also hope for an experience of the transcendent. They hope that meet-ing a God "high and lofty" (Isa. 6:1) will be the means for their encountering the depth dimension they seek.

We are increasingly receiving into our worshiping com-munities people whose hearts have been turned toward God by the Holy Spirit for perhaps the first time. While *we* can trust that it is the Spirit who has drawn them toward the church, *they* have only a vague awareness of who or what it is they seek.

For such individuals, our inherited forms of Christian education simply will not suffice. Most Christian education programs are information-based. At worst, they take the form of an "adult forum," whose topic may as likely be combating high blood pressure as a conversation about the significance of the doctrine of the Trinity for communal life. Even the best Christian education programs are often based on delivering content *about* the faith to that small group of people in the congregation committed to lifelong learning. They are not reaching the congregation as a whole. And they're certainly not meeting the needs of the postmoderns now joining us. It's not *in*formation that they need, but *form*ation.

The Spirit is inviting us to re-envision how we bring people to faith under the more comprehensive rubric of Christian formation. Such a re-envisioning will broaden our imagination and deepen our practices of enculturating new Christians. We will begin to think of worship, small-group ministries, and engagement in mission—as well as more traditional educational programs—as formative processes, shaping new and old converts alike so that they grow to reflect the life of Christ more clearly in their own lives.

Christian formation is a process as old as the church itself. It is the process of helping a person who may initially be drawn only to one aspect of Christian life (for example, those young parents' interest in their children's moral education) discover the depth of life and the full richness of faith the tradition offers. Formation is as much about developing Christian disciplines and practices as it is about gaining knowledge about the Christian tradition. So it will focus on learning to pray and to practice Christian hospitality as much as on learning about the Trinity and the Incarnation. It will focus on integrating what we learn about the faith into the way we live and on helping Christians deepen their life with God in Christ. Over time, it will transform 21st-century pagans into Christians.

New-Member Classes as Christian Formation

A few years ago, Mary Lynn and I realized that our four-session new-member class wasn't offering enough depth for those entering the church through it. As in most mainline churches, we spent a little time in our new-member processes talking about the particularities of our denomination and our congregation and asked people to tell us a little about their own journeys of faith. We finally realized we were assuming a whole body of knowledge and Christian experience that just wasn't there for most people who attended the classes. We were doing a disservice to people who were honestly seeking to connect deeply with Christ through our church.

We decided to design a 10-week new-member process titled "Come and See" (based on Philip's response to Nathaniel's half-cynical, half-curious question, "Can anything good come out of Nazareth?" [John 1:46]). We even asked new members who were lifelong Presbyterians to participate in the class—people who resisted having to go through *any* process to prove their bona fides to a new congregation. We reminded them that they were now at a different place on their journey with Christ than they were the last time they joined a congregation; we invited them to think of the class as an opportunity to reflect on where the Spirit was leading them in this new setting.

The syllabus for the class assumed that at least one or two people in the room will know almost nothing about the faith. They won't have the slightest idea what an "Old Testament" and a "New Testament" are, much less in which of them you'd find Mark. What they know about Jesus will be shaped by the sketchy information about him that still floats through popular culture ("Is 'Christ' his last name?"). Right at the start, Mary Lynn and I encouraged the kind of "small-group" sharing that can build a sense of community. We laid out the ground rules early on that we would all practice confidentiality about what was shared in our conversations, and that there would be no such thing as a "dumb question" in our sessions.

Mary Lynn and I introduced them to the truth claims of scripture through a discussion of Wabash College religion professor William Placher's excellent article "Is the Bible True?," which appeared originally in *The Christian Century*.[1] Placher takes a nonfoundationalist approach to truth with which postmoderns can readily identify. Instead of arguing that the Bible gives us "the" truth about life, Placher instead makes the case that scripture provides a comprehensive way of making sense of life, one that many of us will find makes the *best* sense of our experience. He provides a sophisticated yet flexible enough definition of truth to draw postmoderns into a deeper conversation with scripture and the way of life it recommends.

Having introduced the foundational text of the faith, we next introduced class members to worship, spending one session exploring the meaning of the liturgical year and another going through our weekly order of worship, laying out the theology that lies behind its form and structure. We encouraged people to talk about differences they had discovered between the way we worshiped and prayed and how they had practiced those disciplines in other religious communities. Given the wide variety of worship experiences people brought to the discussion (including none at all), this conversation often flushed out assumptions people make about the nature of worship and the meaning of what we do when we gather to give our thanks and praise to God.

The next session focused on church history. We helped people understand how the wide variety of denominational families developed, as well as the place our own tradition inhabited in that theological landscape. Mary Lynn and I made the point that each denominational stream bears the catholic tradition in a particular way and with particular emphases. Especially as the idea of denominations comes to mean less and less to the average seeker, giving witness to the catholicity of the church gives them permission to value the spiritual practices and understanding about faith they bring with them into our congregation. It will, after all, be far more important in the 21st century for people to be able to say how and why they are *Christian* than it will be for them to be able to explain what it means to be Methodist or Roman Catholic, Baptist or Presbyterian.

While there was, admittedly, a good deal of *in*formation conveyed during these initial sessions, a continuing emphasis on *form*ation also coursed through them. In the session on Scripture, for example, not only did Mary Lynn and I talk about what we meant when we said that scripture is "true"; we also led the class through an experience of *lectio divina*, a slow meditative reading of scripture, and invited participants to begin to practice that discipline. They came back the next week and talked in small groups about what they had experienced as they read scripture meditatively. Having people share their faith in small groups each week gives them an early experience of Christian community and begins to build a level of trust that will make a deeper experience of being part of the body of Christ possible. By honoring one another's faith stories, we practice hospitality and begin to regard one another as sisters and brothers in Christ.

The second half of the 10-week series became even more focused on spiritual disciplines, both individual and corporate. We spent a couple of weeks talking about what Richard Foster, a best-selling author on spiritual formation, refers to the "inner" disciplines as prayer, devotional study of scripture and other spiritual classics of the faith, and spiritual direction. During these sessions, Sandra, director of the Christian formation center that is part of our church's ministry, led the class through a "taste" of several forms of prayer and talked about opportunities for individual spiritual direction and Christian formation seminars offered through the center. The next two sessions focused on some of the practices Foster calls the "outer" spiritual disciplines—living a life of faithful stewardship, engaging in mission and service in the name of Christ, and becoming aware of one's vocation. Pastors and members of our church board talked about opportunities for engaging in Christ's mission through the congregation's life. Lay leaders explained how they understood the work they did Monday through Friday to be their vocation. (If we really believe in the priesthood of all believers, we've got to stop applying the term "vocation" only to ordained ministers.) They told how they had grown to understand stewardship as a way of living in thankful response to God's gifts, a response involving far more than making a pledge to the church's operating budget.

Although we often encountered initial resistance to such a long new-member reception process, inevitably we heard from at least half of each class that it was a great experience. More than a couple of people in each group would eagerly ask, "What's next?" In fact, the congregation has begun to think about developing two 10-week follow-up classes, one focusing on the basic doctrines of the Christian faith and the other exploring spiritual disciplines in more depth. The people coming into our congregations are eager for an in-depth enculturation into the faith. Offering them anything less fails to take seriously the longing with which they come into our communities.

Confirmation as Christian Formation

Most studies of the continuing decline in membership in mainline churches point out that the problem is *not* that we are losing members to more evangelical churches. Rather, we are losing members who "slip out the back door" of the church and into the ranks of those not attending any church. A key moment in this process often occurs when young people who have been nurtured in the bosom of the church from childhood leave for college. Every pastor I know has more than a fair share of tales of woe told by parents who mourn their young-adult children's departure from the faith community.

We have failed to form the faith of many of our youth sufficiently to help them withstand the critique of that faith they will inevitably encounter in most American universities and colleges. This ought to be a clear enough signal to us that our present forms of Christian education for children and youth, no matter how wonderful they are, are not up to the task. But neither have traditional catechism processes sufficiently shaped our youth to keep them connected to their faith in young adulthood. Something more substantial is required for the skeptical cultural context in which we live.

We were fortunate to have as our youth ministers a married couple who took not only their own spiritual journeys seriously but also the journeys of the young people with whom they worked. Wendy is in a Ph.D. program in Christian spirituality. Both George and Wendy have recently made the decision to embrace the Roman Catholic tradition, and have gone through its yearlong rite of Christian initiation for adults (RCIA) before being received into membership in a nearby parish.

As the members of the staff responsible for overseeing youth confirmation, they decided to stretch what had formerly been a six- to eight-week information-based class into a nine-month invitation to Christian formation. They modified the basic RCIA structure to make it more developmentally appropriate for young adults and adapted its content to reflect a Reformed/Presbyterian rather than a Roman Catholic tradition. Every session began with *lectio divina*. George and Wendy assumed that the youth wanted to wrestle seriously with the content of the faith as well and invited them into serious theological conversation as they met together.

Not every young person who went through this process made a profession of faith at its conclusion. We were far more confident, however, that every participant had a strong foundation—intellectually and devotionally—from which eventually to make the decision to follow in the way of Christ.

Rethinking Christian Education

An interesting thing happened along the way of our developing the "Come and See" new-member classes. Some members of our church board went through the series as hosts. They came out of the experience saying they had learned more about the faith during those 10 weeks than they had in any other Christian education offering. They began to develop a vision for reconceptualizing our Christian education program as a ministry of Christian formation.

One of the lines in the Davis congregation's vision statement says that it is a church "that engages both the head and the heart in the journey of faith." Even with that stated intention, though, it had been a difficult struggle for us to find that purported balance. This was a university church, so its members loved to "think the faith" to death. However, we became increasingly aware over the years what a lopsided form of faith such an unbalanced approach produces. It's like deciding to work with free weights at the gym, but working out only the muscles on the left side of the body. The resulting physique doesn't have much to recommend it. Beginning to think in terms of Christian formation helped us— in fact as well as in hope—to engage our hearts as fully as our heads in the practice of faith.

We started with our youngest children, having incorporated Episcopal Christian educator Jerome Berryman's "Godly Play" curriculum into our Sunday school design. "Godly Play" presents the stories of the Bible in language and concepts developmentally appropriate for young children. It employs a Montessori-like approach, inviting children to interact with the stories imaginatively and through movement as they explore the physical materials used to help narrate the Bible stories. Not only do they learn the stories, but in addition, their imaginations are shaped. They begin to learn how to see the world through Christian lenses. They learn how to "be" Christian in the world.

We also adapted our Christian education for older children to include their parents in a family-based formation process. Sandra was inspired to design a class called "Faith Family Clusters" when she began to hear parents say, "Judy came home from Sunday school today and said they talked about prayer. She asked me, 'Daddy, how do you pray?' I didn't have a clue how to respond." Parents, as well as children, were asking Sandra about basic practices of the faith and wanted to learn how to develop those practices as a family, not just individually.

Sandra realized we needed a formation process that would help parents and children (and sometimes even grandparents—have you noticed how many grandparents are raising their grandchildren these days?) to experience what it would mean to be a Christian family in today's world. She developed a three-year curriculum focused more on formation than on information. Each class introduced Christian rituals that could be used at home: grace at meals, family prayer times, and the celebration of baptismal anniversaries. Following an opening ritual, the first half of each class session was spent in intergenerational conversation about the theme of the day; for example, baptism or the meaning of Advent. During the second half of the class, the children went to one part of the room and the adults to another, so that each could continue to explore the theme in ways that were developmentally appropriate. Major feasts of the Christian year and each person's birthday and baptismal anniversary were celebrated.

We also shifted the focus of our youth and adult-education offerings, so that at any given time we were offering classes on developing spiritual disciplines as well as classes teaching *about* the faith. We began to develop two "tracks" in our Christian formation program. One was aimed toward providing basic introductory classes for people new to the faith (the class "Bonehead Bible" is a continuing favorite). The other provided classes that delved deeper into the faith for those who were already on the road with Jesus and seeking to go further along it. Each track included classes in which meditative reading of the Bible was practiced and classes in which a critical reading of the biblical text was emphasized. Our Christian formation center's offerings throughout the week came to be seen as essential complements to our traditional Sunday morning education hour. Many topics and practices can't be adequately covered in the typical 50-minute class on a packed-schedule Sunday morning. The center's offerings typically allowed more time to explore the subject or practice under consideration.

Developing a Center for Christian Formation

One of the greatest gifts the Davis congregation gave its staff members was permission to serve the congregation with their own spiritual gifts and sense of call. While each of us was called with a particular job description in mind, the church's leaders were amazingly flexible about letting us follow the lead of the Spirit as our ministries in this congregation developed.

Perhaps one of the most amazing of those journeys was Sandra Lommasson's 27-year tenure on our staff. She served as director of the weekday nursery school, director of Christian education, minister with families, and minister of Christian formation. She is now director of the Bread of Life Center, the Christian formation center housed at the Davis church facilities. While given birth by our congregation, the center was shared ecumenically with churches not only in our town but also in the surrounding metro region. In many ways, the narrative of her journey through these many job descriptions illustrates that congregation's shift from a traditional Christian education program to its current focus on Christian formation.

The center's ministry grew out of Sandra's experience of people in the parish coming to her asking for help in their prayer life just at the moment she was feeling called by God to deepen her own devotional life. Deciding she needed to learn more about prayer, she went through a spiritual-direction training program offered by the Sisters of Mercy, a Roman Catholic order (this was before Protestant seminaries began offering programs in spiritual direction).

As Sandra started a ministry of spiritual direction "on the side," along with her oversight of our Christian education ministry, our congregational leaders began to sense that this was not only God's call to her but also God's call to the congregation as a whole. We went through a formal process of discernment over a couple of years, first among the pastoral staff and then in our church board. The board decided to ask Sandra to establish a center for Christian formation in a space in the church that had providentially been underutilized for years.

A little more than five years later, the center has seven spiritual directors on its staff from four denominations. It offers an expansive schedule of seminars for both laity and pastors, and trains spiritual directors for ministries throughout the Central Valley of California. An ecumenical advisory board with both Protestant and Roman Catholic members oversees its ministry, though the center remains formally a part of the Davis church's ministry. What began as one Christian's call to deepen her own prayer life has become a ministry that is helping to shape hundreds of Christian communities.

An Ongoing Transformation

Although we had been trying to implement a ministry of Christian formation for more than a decade in our congregation, we still found it easy to slip back into a default concept of Christian education. It still took a great deal of mindfulness and intention to remind ourselves to include enough emphasis on formation in our offerings for children, youth, and adults. We continued to believe that there was a role for informational learning as well as formational experience in our overall ministry, but we were not always sure what the balance between or the sequencing of the two ought to be. Clearly it's going to take the congregation longer than another decade to work its way out of the older, inherited models of Christian education and to develop a more holistic model for enculturating people into Christian faith and life.

But the responses we got from people told us we were on the right track. Younger seekers told us they "got" what we were trying to show them as well as what we were trying to teach them. They talked about feeling that they were really growing in their faith, that they were becoming followers of Christ. Older members described the greater depth they discovered in their life of faith. They spoke of deriving as much meaning from the Christian meditation class in which they practiced various disciplines of prayer as they did from the class in which they explored several approaches to biblical interpretation. Thinking about the faith and experiencing the faith came together as ways to draw closer to God.

CHAPTER 5

Being Drawn into the Mission of God

Postmoderns are searching for worship in which they experience God's presence and are helped to give God their thanks and praise. Introducing them to spiritual practices, as well as to the church's theological tradition and its unique way of seeing the world, will draw them closer to God and begin forming them into followers of Christ. But if that's all your congregation does for them, they still may not stick around. Gen X and younger Christians are also interested in finding a place to commit their lives and to make a difference in the world.

These younger seekers especially disdain the "me generation" attitude that marked the baby boomer cohort, which now holds positions of leadership in many of our congregations. They believe the boomer generation's self-absorption has left the planet's resources depleted and American society impoverished. "You took and took," they will say to people my age, "but you never gave anything back." Younger Americans want to give their lives to a project greater than providing for their own comfort and ease, and they come to the church hoping that we will challenge them to join such a project.

Neither are they interested in simply providing for the congregation's life and ministry, taking care of its own internal needs. Therefore, the most deadly thing we can do initially with a postmodern Christian is to stick her on a committee. That's definitely not the kind of community or the kind of service in which these folk are interested. In fact, if we don't challenge them to change the world, they'll slip out the back door of the church, no matter how awe-inspiring our worship is or how deeply we encourage them to develop their walk with Christ.

They are not interested in the kind of checkbook mission that has become the mainstay of many of our affluent mainline congregations. For them, it is not enough to send money to support the mission of the denomination or to help finance the local soup kitchen or homeless shelter. Postmoderns want to send *themselves*, not just their dollars, into mission. They are looking for ways to become directly involved in working for justice, providing acts of hospitality and service, and offering healing to those in need. They want to "proclaim the year of the Lord's favor" (Luke 4:19), as Jesus did—by performing direct acts of healing, hospitality, and hope.

Two New Ways to Think of Mission

Two movements that have developed over the past several years have provided tremendous insights to Davis Community Church's leaders and members as they have thought through how to develop the direct style of mission for which postmodern Christians are yearning.

The Once and Future Church

The first is the "once and future church" movement developed by Alban Institute founder Loren Mead in his book *The Once and Future Church*[1] and later expanded into a whole series of books on that theme. Mead made the case that Christianity has lived through two great paradigms for understanding the relationship between itself and the world and is now beginning to enter a third.

The first was the Apostolic paradigm, when the church was a tiny minority surrounded by a decidedly hostile world. The second was the Christendom paradigm. It began with Constantine's establishment of Christianity as the state religion of the Roman Empire and was marked by a breakdown in the barrier between the church and the surrounding culture, so that the whole world (at least the West) was declared to be a Christian realm. Under the Christendom paradigm, the state and the wider culture broadly supported the church, its worldview, and its work.

While Mead was reluctant to name the third paradigm for the church's existence into which we are now moving, it has many affinities with the emerging church I have described. Because he believed we are in the early phases of this emerging church, he was fairly modest in his description of the dawning context for the church's ministry. "Neither the new age nor the new paradigm has arrived," Mead warned, "so we are pulled by the new and constrained by the old without the privilege even of knowing fully what the new will be like."[2] His words ring true for those of us clergy who serve during this time between the paradigms, and who believe we will not be in ministry long enough to see the final shape of the emerging church.

Mead did, however, make the clear claim that the shift toward the emerging church means that we need radically to rethink our understanding of mission, especially to rethink where we believe the mission field begins. In the Christendom paradigm, in which the culture surrounding the church is understood to be firmly part of the realm of God, the mission field is at the edge of the empire. Missionaries are people sent to that frontier to convert nonbelievers and to bring them into the fold. It's been a long time since there was anything like the Holy Roman Empire. And yet Christians in America continued to live out of the Christendom paradigm for mission until quite recently. A favorite periodical for many mainline Christians, *The Christian Century,* was, in fact, named on the assumption that the 20th century would be the century when Christianity spread from its Western base to cover the whole world. Most denominations downsized their home mission agencies because leaders believed that America had been completely converted. "Mission" came to be understood primarily as what we did to take the gospel to the far corners of the earth.

Now all that has changed, Mead said. Not only should we admit the hubris that led us to believe that America was a Christian nation in the first place. We also need to banish the notion that the call of mission is for "us" to send the gospel to "them," especially when the people we think of as "them" are far away. Mead asserted that the present situation of the American church was more akin to the church in the Apostolic era than to the church of the 1940s. Not only is the surrounding culture *not* thoroughly Christian. It has, in the minds of many theologians and missiologists, become "repaganized," if we mean by that term that it has become a culture whose values and worldview are shaped by forces other than the Christian vision. In part, this means that the mission field is no longer at the edge of the empire but—as in the Apostolic paradigm—immediately outside the front doors of our churches.

When we begin to shift the focus to mission "on our doorstep," as Mead described our present call, we find ourselves invited to carry out the very kinds of direct mission to which postmoderns want to commit their lives. There are plenty of hurting people right outside our sanctuaries. There is plenty to do in our own communities to give witness to the love of Christ, the healing power the church offers in Christ's name, and the justice that marks the realm of God. There are plenty of places in which we can invite these new Christians to become involved in mission.

The Missional Church

In response to discussion instituted by the British missiologist Bishop Lesslie Newbigin, an ecumenical group of American missiologists began in the late 1980s what they named the "Gospel and Our Culture Network." The network includes Princeton Seminary professor Darrell Guder and South American missiologist David Bosch. They launched the network with the assumption that the church in North America had become so disestablished that it was necessary to speak again of our own continent as a mission field. Given that context, these missiologists said we needed completely to rethink how we talk about mission, about taking the gospel into that estranged culture. Rather than speaking of the mission of the *church* (a model more suited to Mead's Christendom paradigm) they spoke of the church's being invited into the *missio Dei,* the mission of *God.* In their foundational book *Missional Church,* a group of authors led by editor Darrell Guder wrote, "We have come to see that mission is not merely an activity of the church. Rather, mission is the result of God's initiative, rooted in God's purposes to restore and heal creation."[3] In the authors' understanding, the church is not the *goal* of God's mission but its *instrument* (that is, the church is the *means,* not the *end,* of God's purposes). The church exists for mission, for taking the good news about Jesus Christ into a hurting world and to assist in what the Jewish community refers to as "the repair of the world."

The network named three aspects of the vocation of the church as it enters into the *missio Dei.* The church is called and sent to represent the reign of God: to be a people sent on a mission, to act faithfully on behalf of the reign of God in the public sphere, and to speak of that reign "in post-Christendom accents as confident yet humble messengers of the reign of God."[4] The church is called to be the apostle to the world, bearing a distinctively Christian culture and worldview into an alien landscape. And the church is to cultivate communities of the Holy Spirit whose members bear the particular marks of a Christian vocabulary, Christian values, and commitment to the reign of God. Each of these aspects of the church's missional vocation presumes an unmistakable difference between the church in North America and its surrounding culture. Like Mead, these missiologists understood our primary mission field to be immediately at our doorstep. As we begin to shift our emphasis from maintaining the institution of the church toward employing its resources for mission to the surrounding culture, we will begin to make commitments that, again, will attract postmodern seekers with their desire to make a real difference in the world.

A New Missional Context

The relatively affluent Davis congregation's mission emphasis had focused on supporting our denomination's world-
wide mission and our presbytery's regional mission. We were
comfortably able to provide for our own ministry (for example, for salaries, utilities, and upkeep of facilities) and,
therefore, had extra funds that we could donate toward mission "out there." Mission, in our minds, was a calling for
someone else, somewhere else. As we began to listen carefully to people like Loren Mead and the Gospel and Our
Culture Network, however, we discovered a whole host of
opportunities for mission on our doorstep into which we
could send postmodern missionaries. We also discovered
some of the difficulties that come with living, as Mead put it,
in the time between the paradigms.

One difficulty Mead noted in our present situation is that
while we are beginning to recognize that a hurting, pagan
culture lies just beyond our doorstep, we continue to have a
hard time helping our own members see that the mission
field is right outside the sanctuary doors. It's hard for them
to discern any missional boundary there, any distinction between the values of the church and the values of the culture.
They move back and forth across that boundary without
noting much difference. This lack of perception is due in part
to the lingering echoes of Christian values in American culture and in part to our failure to form Christians who recognize the difference between the two cultures. But as we
undertake a more thoroughgoing process of formation with
new Christians, especially with new postmodern Christians,
they are likely to "get" that difference more clearly than
longer-time parish members. They are more likely to see the
difference between the two cultures because they come to us
clearly understanding that American culture no longer bears
distinctively Christian markings. The more postmoderns who
join our churches, therefore, the more clarity the church as a
whole will have about the boundary between its worldview
and values and those of the surrounding culture.

As we emphasize the growing difference between church and culture and give our parishioners experiences that help them to *sense* that difference, they will be more likely to recognize the mission opportunities that lie all around us. And the greater their awareness of our new setting for mission, the greater the likelihood that they will be drawn by the Spirit to take on those opportunities to engage in the *missio Dei* in our own backyard.

Examples of Mission at the Doorstep

One of the most important ways we began to discover mission at our doorstep was to pay attention to those who lived just outside it. By attending to neighbors just beyond the borders of our church property, whether or not they ever risked setting a foot inside the church, we began to find people to whom God was sending us.

Getting to Know the Homeless

Because Davis Community Church is in the downtown area of Davis and across the street from its principal park, we always had homeless people as our neighbors. For years, the church quietly allowed the occasional homeless individual to sleep on the church grounds to get in out of the wind or the rain. Several years ago, however, we decided to develop a more intentional relationship with the homeless community at our doorstep. We began providing lunches out of our church office five days a week for anyone who stopped by. Word got out on the street quickly, and we soon had a steady flow of people through the office each noon. Once it became evident that the people asking for lunches were comfortable coming into our space, both pastors and office staff began introducing themselves to the homeless folk and asking them to tell us a bit of their stories. Their reactions to our interest made it clear that for many of them, never in recent memory had someone treated them as real human beings rather than as bums. Over time they began to share more and more of their stories, so that we developed genuine friendships with a number of the homeless. They began to trust us and to come to us with problems they faced. We learned about the circumstances that had led them to life on the road. We knew we had made a significant breakthrough when a couple of them came to ask Mary Lynn if she would officiate at a memorial service they wanted to hold for a friend who had died of alcoholism.

We stumbled at one point, however. We began to let it be known more widely that people were welcome to sleep on the church property. We had an evening custodian who was a father figure of sorts to a number of individuals in the local homeless community, and he was willing to provide some oversight to make sure everyone was safely bedded down. For the homeless who call our community more or less their permanent home, the arrangement worked well. But homeless people passing through town learned of our offer and also began to sleep over on the church grounds. That was not a problem, in and of itself, but they were less committed to following the few rules we had laid down to make sure our hospitality didn't cause problems for the folk who lived across the street from the church. After several nights of shouting and a few fights among the more transient overnight visitors, we were soon being asked to meet with angry and anxious neighbors.

We finally realized that we had not thought through the issues systemically enough. In our desire to practice hospitality to the homeless community, we had failed to think through our need to practice hospitality to the homeowners across the street. Eventually, we had to ask people to stop sleeping on the grounds, though they are still welcome to be in and around the church during the day. We also realized we had failed to invite the homeless explicitly to consider themselves part of our community. Something in us still thought of them as an outside group with whom we were involved in mission rather than as people Jesus had invited into the Christian community with us.

Given our successes and our stumbles, we realized we needed to think more deeply about the kind of mission that

God had invited us to extend to our homeless neighbors. The church now has a task force that has been working with the city, the neighbors, and other interested community organizations to establish an emergency cold-weather shelter in town. While it isn't severely cold for long during Davis winters, there is still a short period when shelter could be a life-or-death matter. Our church board decided to take the lead in the community to advocate for such a shelter and to offer our facilities as one of the locations to be considered for that shelter. We began more consistently to invite homeless individuals to join us for worship or to participate in the life of our congregation than we did before. We learned more about the middle-class assumptions and fears that keep us from fully accepting the homeless as brothers and sisters in Christ. It was not always an easy or comfortable process, but we discovered how to be in mission on our doorstep with the homeless community.

The Art of Public Reconciliation

For many years the Davis congregation had an unspoken rule about welcoming gay and lesbian people into its community life: they were welcome as long as we didn't have to talk about their sexual orientation. Amid our denomination's most recent round of debates on sexual orientation and ordination, however, our church board felt called by the Spirit to be clearer about the welcome we wanted to extend. Mary Lynn and I had asked a number of people in the congregation to consider applying for a youth-ministry position. Among those we invited was a bisexual woman who had already done great work with the kids in our church, and who was well loved by them. Eventually she declined the opportunity out of concern that her sexual orientation might become an issue with some youths' parents. When our church board realized that she felt unable to respond to a call even to a nonordained position of leadership, board members felt called to tackle the issue head-on. They voted to enter what turned out to be a more-than-yearlong process of learning about homosexuality and about the Christian understanding of

sexual orientation. At the close of that process the board decided to extend a public welcome to all people, regardless of
sexual orientation, into the full life and ministry of the congregation. I won't pretend that the process was without pain:
it's hard for a Christian community to look such a poten-
tially divisive issue squarely in the face. But we were confident that we had done all we could to discern the will of
God for our congregation through that process.

Now known publicly as a congregation that had declared
its openness to gays and lesbians, we found ourselves invited to take a leadership role in a mission of reconciliation
in the broader community. Being a university town, Davis
has a sizable and politically vocal gay and lesbian community (whose current preferred designation is "GLBT," an ab-
breviation for "gay, lesbian, bisexual, transgendered"). The
Davis city council passed a civil rights ordinance for gays
and lesbians back in the 1980s and prides itself on being a
diverse and inclusive community. Through a land swap with
the University of California at Davis, the city became owner
of a Boy Scout cabin built years ago by the local Rotary Club.
What began as a discussion in the council's human relations
commission about the city's new landlord relationship with
a Boy Scout troop soon turned into a nasty public battle over
the national Scouting policy that excludes gay men and boys
from Scouting. Leaders of the local Scouting community, on
the one hand, and leaders of the local gay and lesbian community, on the other, began employing extremely destructive
tactics. The debate became so divisive that longtime friendships were being lost—friendships among people who, in
the past, had together provided much leadership for our city.

Our church held a unique position in the community,
because we had both publicly welcomed gays and lesbians
and sponsored three Scouting units. I was approached by a
few leaders from each side of the issue and asked to convene
an informal conversation about how the issues raised could
be resolved without damaging long-term relationships important for the city's future. We spent weeks just lowering
tensions and calming emotions enough for a civil conversa-

tion to begin. Over the course of a year, I was able to help the leaders on both sides discover their common commitment to serving the youth of our community and to working for a more inclusive Scouting program. Eventually Mary Lynn and I helped them develop a common resolution to the Davis city council to work toward those ends. The issue still flares up from time to time, but our willingness to be agents of reconciliation in the surrounding community provided us an unexpected opportunity to work with God in the desire to bring healing to the whole world.

While this was a difficult discussion for some of our older members, our postmodern members enthusiastically ap-plauded their pastors' public role in the reconciliation pro-cess. Having been raised with a more diverse and inclusive set of friends than their parents (and certainly their grand-parents) had been, they wanted the church to work for a more fully inclusive community both within the church and in the wider culture. A number of those postmodern congregants came to Mary Lynn and me during that process and said, "This is *exactly* the sort of thing the church ought to be doing in the community."

Failures as Well as Successes

We learned about mission at our doorstep through our fail-ures as well as through our successes. Our Bread of Life Cen-ter for Christian Formation was the first religious nonprofit group to seek a grant from our local county government's welfare-to-work program. Our church had entered an ear-lier process of discerning where God might be calling us, as a congregation, to be in mission in our city. In that process, we discovered that many people trying to get off welfare and into the workforce had many places they could go to get help with individual issues and barriers they faced in that process. But we also learned that the delivery system for those services was fractured, so that many clients became discour-aged and ended up dropping out of the welfare-to-work pro-gram. Our proposal for a Family Mentoring Program, which was funded for a trial year by the county board of supervisors, sought to pair mentors from the faith communities of Davis with clients in the welfare-to-work process. Our plan was to pair each welfare client with a friend and mentor who would not only walk with the client through the often frustrating process but also could help coach him or her in the life skills many clients needed to develop to succeed in the world of work.

We discovered some of the deficiencies in our design almost immediately. First, we were unable to find enough mentors willing to give the time and to put up with the frustration of working with people who had multiple social problems. We learned the hard way how thoroughly enculturated most of our members were to asking "What's in it for me and mine?" when considering involvement in the church. We also learned how leery government agencies can be of religious institutions undertaking a public mission. Even though the county had given us the money for this mission effort, the county staff repeatedly resisted cooperating with our efforts to reach out to potential clients. Their fear of breaching the wall of separation between church and state, as they understood that wall, kept them from giving us the access we needed to make contact with the clients who would benefit most from the one-on-one relationship we were offering. Because of both factors, we were not able to meet the quantitative goals written into the grant contract. Many a job seeker whose life we were able to touch, however, was transformed through the relationship with a mentor and went on to make a successful transition off welfare.

A Still Developing Paradigm

The shift away from thinking about mission as something the church does in faraway places and toward imagining ourselves stepping just outside our own sanctuary doors to enter the mission field represents a major change in perspective for most of our congregations. The boundary between congregation and world is still too indistinct. Most of our members don't see any conflict in living comfortably in both worlds. Although Loren Mead said he was convinced that mission at the doorstep might be the clearest invitation to the church arising out of his "third paradigm," it will take another generation or two before that invitation is clearly heard by our congregations as a whole.

But the more aware our parishioners become that the culture around us champions values different from those we derive from our faith, the more they will consider it their primary arena for entering the *missio Dei*. The postmoderns in our congregations will grasp that divergence most quickly. They grew up with the values of the larger culture. They have chosen to come into the church as a countercultural act, to take a stand against the values of the wider culture and on the side of the values of the Christian community. They will lead us into these new mission fields with their shared commitment to making a difference in the world. This arena of church life may be the one in which our postmodern members will most naturally take the lead in helping us discern the shape of the emerging church.

CHAPTER 6

Leadership in the Emerging Church

Unless we have founded a brand-new nondenominational church, each of us has inherited a polity from our congregation's denominational tradition. Be it a hierarchical, connectional, or congregational polity, the ways we exercise leadership and make decisions for the congregation as a whole are guided by some form of canon law, discipline, or constitution.

Aristotle argued that the whole point of having a *polis* is to form its members into better people than they would be, had they not been members of that *polis*. A Christian polity, then, ought to focus on forming communities whose members are better human beings because they now know themselves in the light of what God has done in Jesus Christ. The primary model for our polities, then, is the polity that Jesus himself instituted among the Twelve, a form of community that the early church sought to replicate in its own life. It was a polity that focused on the values of the realm of God, and in which adherents practiced radically inclusive table fellowship, held up the words and acts of Jesus as exemplars of the Christian life, and sought above all to be a community shaped by their love for one another.

Christians with postmodern sensibilities will bring a new set of questions to bear on how the polities we have inherited do and don't help us form such a community in the emerging church. In particular, they will bring a helpful critique of past instances in which the church borrowed concepts from other polities to help shape its self-understanding—

other polities that may be less congruent with that of Jesus than we might ordinarily think.

Borrowing from Other Polities

I want to focus on three areas of church polity that we have borrowed—sometimes consciously, sometimes unconsciously—from other polities. They are aspects of our polities ripe for critique by postmoderns:

- the administrative and corporate focus of our polities,
- the adversarial nature of our reliance on parliamentary procedure, and
- the professional status we have granted clergy.

Administrative and Corporate Focus

Once Constantine adopted Christianity as the state religion of the Roman Empire, the church quickly became another administrative organization in the emperor's service. The rubric "one emperor, one church" became the guiding principle for every level of governance throughout the empire. The church was organized into dioceses and parishes whose boundaries closely matched those of the empire's administrative units, and the goals of empire and church were understood to be the same.

The dissolution of the Roman Empire—and, with it, any sense of "one church"—and the rise of denominationalism in the Western church in the aftermath of the Reformation has certainly diluted our role in service to the secular state. In the United States, with its Jeffersonian understanding of the separation of church and state, that relationship has become even more attenuated—at least formally. Until quite recently, however, the church still enjoyed a privileged role in the wider community and was broadly understood to be supportive of the goals of the nation.

Wary of all monolithic structures and especially of the power such structures can exert, postmodern Christians increasingly are questioning whether the church has *any* role in supporting the national polity. They are drawn to the kinds of alternate polities for church communities championed by theologians and church leaders influenced by Karl Barth, the Swiss theologian. Barth called for the church to be a distinctive community that drew its cues for the shape of its life from the gospel of Jesus Christ rather than from any other source. Duke Divinity School professors Stanley Hauerwas and William H. Willimon have taken up Barth's cause.[1] In their books about "resident aliens," they insist that the most important political act the church can take is to become a *polis* shaped by the narrative of God's saving acts in Israel and, finally, in Jesus Christ.

Younger seekers come to us looking for an alternative to the life they know outside the church. They look at American life and see a culture whose primary aim is to shape people into consumers. American polity tends to shape individuals who have little interest in relationships (beyond finding the occasional partner for good sex) and little hope that the world is not quickly going to hell in a handbasket. When they come into our sanctuaries, they are hoping to find something other than a community that understands itself to be providing theological support to that broader secular polity. To postmoderns, providing support for the wider culture seems akin to rearranging the deck chairs on the Titanic. Like Barth, they don't want the church to be a slightly nicer form of the world. They want the church to be the church in a way that clearly distinguishes it from the broader culture.

Over the course of the 20th century, American denominations often turned to the world of business to borrow models for structuring their operations, much as they turned to the Roman Empire for structural models following the Constantinian establishment. Denominations began to look more and more like corporations, with congregations serving as their local franchises. Pastors began to think of their congregations as small nonprofit businesses for which they were to serve as CEOs.

In my own Presbyterian tradition, much has been written about how our denomination has changed from a mission agency to a regulatory bureaucracy. One pastor I know, a student of the history of our denomination's constitution, says that until almost the mid-20th century, the predecessor to *The Book of Order* of today could fit easily in a shirt pocket. It focused on broad principles for church governance and left it to the discretion of individual judicatories to find ways to apply those principles to particular issues that arose within their bounds. Now, however, *The Book of Order* has turned into quite a hefty tome, full of language that sounds far more like the Federal Register than it does the U.S. Constitution, far more regulatory than principled.

In part, the adoption of a more regulatory approach to church organization is a sign of the breakdown of theological consensus in the denomination as a whole. Since different parties in the PCUSA no longer trust one another to exercise discretionary powers in accordance with the gospel, they seek to mandate what all should do. Perhaps more telling, though, is that most Presbyterians have come to think of church judicatories as regulatory agencies. Judicatories, then, live up to these expectations and do what regulatory agencies do—micromanage the life of their franchises (just as McDonald's tells its franchisees exactly how each menu item should be prepared and packaged). The result, even in a polity that formally is understood to have a bottom-up form of governance, is a top-down authority that demands compliance from the judicatories lower in the denomination's structures.

Gen X and younger Christians have a knee-jerk reaction against such a regulatory, top-down system of governance and its heavy-handed authority. If authority is to be broadly shared—one of postmoderns' cherished principles—then it must be exercised as locally as possible. They want local communities to be trusted to make decisions consistent with the general principles that bind a particular tradition together, but in a way that still allows for local concerns and perspectives. Churches that take a bureaucratic approach to church governance will find themselves handicapped in the emerging church, because postmoderns will go where their voices can be heard and their understanding of God's will can be part of the decision-making mix, whether or not they're part of the formal leadership structure.

Adversarial Decision Making

Most of our polities, somewhere in their constitutional documents, will tell us that we are to use the latest version of *Robert's Rules of Order* in our decision making, whether at the level of a local church board or a national convocation. *Robert's Rules* does bring order to our sometimes messy debates and decision making in church gatherings, but is it really congruent with the sort of community we seek to build in the emerging church?

We may not realize that an American general developed *Robert's Rules* during a lull in the 19th-century Pacific Northwest boundary war between the United States and Canada. He wanted to develop a way for adversaries in a democratic polity to settle their differences by peaceful means. What we need to understand from this short history lesson is that the parliamentary procedure set out in *Robert's Rules* assumes an *adversarial* relationship between the parties seeking to come to a decision. It also favors the energetic extroverts in the room and tends to leave the insights of quieter and more introverted individuals out of the debate.

Admittedly, many decisions in the life of a congregation or judicatory are simple or minor enough that they can appropriately be decided through parliamentary procedure and its "50-percent-plus-one" majority rule. But the more important decisions a congregation or church board faces—for example, those that test the limits of our theological agreement or the boundaries of our table fellowship—do not lend themselves so easily to *Robert's* efficient and winner-take-all rubrics.

Chuck Olsen has paired with Danny Morris to encourage us to employ models of discernment when faced with such important issues.[2] Drawing especially on the discernment processes of Ignatius Loyola, founder of the Jesuits, and on the practices of the Society of Friends, they have developed a process of discernment for use by church boards and judicatories. Their discernment process emphasizes hearing all voices that need to be heard, connecting the issue under consideration with the biblical narrative and the great tradition of the church, and seeking insofar as possible to arrive at consensus. New Testament professor Luke Timothy Johnson of Emory University's Candler School of Theology provides a more thorough biblical grounding for discernment in his book *Scripture and Discernment*.[3]

Discernment, as a method of making important decisions in the life of the church, is a process attuned to postmodern sensibilities. Its emphasis on hearing many voices spreads the authority in decision making broadly throughout the community rather than centering it in the pastor, moderator, or president of a board, or in a few forceful, extroverted leaders. Its use of scripture, tradition, and prayer as its primary tools for moving the conversation forward resonates with postmoderns' interest in a polity that doesn't simply mirror what they find in the broader culture. Its emphasis on the common voice of the community rather than on the few dominant voices that can drive a parliamentary process harmonizes with postmoderns' emphasis on the communal over the individual. And its emphasis on reaching consensus can lead to a sense that the community is seeking to find the will of God rather than merely the will of the majority. Discernment is attractive to postmoderns because of its appeal to the whole person and the whole community when important decisions are being made, and because of the way it distributes power widely in the decision-making process.

The Professionalization of the Clergy

Ask any gathering of clergy whether they do or don't like to be thought of as professionals, and you'll get a widely split vote—with many of the clergy voting both yes *and* no. Certainly some aspects of thinking of clergy as professionals are salutary; for example, the specialized education we ask them to undergo or the standards of accountability we ask them to accept.

Thinking of the clergy leader as the "professional Christian" in a congregation, however, can have unintended detrimental effects on the life of the Christian community. Considering clergy the experts in all matters religious, especially in tandem with thinking of them as the CEOs of congregations, can lead parishioners to think of pastors as a different type of Christian. Such thinking distances clergy from the rest of the congregation and belies our professed belief in the priesthood of all believers. Without meaning to, we constantly reinforce that distancing in church life. In many of our polities the same individual

- preaches regularly to the community and administers its sacraments;
- presides over its administrative board;
- serves as head of staff (a term that, interestingly enough, doesn't even appear in our denomination's constitution);
- heads the church corporation as president, at least in the eyes of the state; and
- answers to the question, "Where does the buck stop?"

No wonder we clergy are considered "professional Christians"!

Even having an educated clergy—a positive hallmark in most traditions—can get in the way of our developing a polity in which each member feels herself or himself to have equal standing as a member of the community and a child of God. For all the insight into scripture it has provided us, I believe few things have done more to distance clergy from laity than the dominance during the past half-century of historical-critical methods of biblical interpretation. Widespread use of these methods has had the unintended consequence of leaving most laity believing that they cannot interpret scripture without a "professional" telling them what the text "really" means. By our heavy reliance on historical-critical methods in our preaching and teaching, we have—certainly unintentionally—tended to cut our parishioners off from the life-giving resource of scripture.

Postmoderns come into the church with a deep mistrust of so-called experts. They don't want their pastor (or anyone else) to be the community's "professional Christian." Their experience tells them that experts have led them more often into danger than into enlightenment. They quickly transfer their wariness about government leaders, corporate executives, leading scientists, and university administrators directly onto clergy. They are wary of giving any one person as much power and authority as our formal and informal pastoral roles in the life of the congregation regularly grant us. They are eager to hear what we have to say about the faith, but they don't want ours to be the only voice they hear. They want to know what others in the community think about the biblical text studied or the theological point expressed. There *are* important roles they want us to play in their life of faith, but being the "professional Christian" isn't one of them.

Our Experiment with Discernment

While I could give examples of the changes Davis Community Church has tried to make in the congregation's life in response to each of the three issues discussed above, I want to focus on an experience of discernment that our church board went through several years ago. I want to offer this example, in particular, for two reasons:

- It ends up addressing all three issues (administrative and corporate focus, adversarial procedure, and the professionalization of clergy).
- It was the experience that jump-started our leadership's process of discerning the outlines of the emerging church.

Mary Lynn and I knew that the ordination of gay and lesbian people was an issue with which our church board needed to wrestle, because more gay and lesbian Christians were finding us a welcoming congregation. They brought with them gifts for leadership that we wanted to invite them to use in our church. Besides, our own study of scripture and the literature on homosexuality had led both Mary Lynn and me to believe that our national church's policy on the issue was wrong. And our denomination had asked its sessions to study the issue for three years and to provide input for the General Assembly at the end of that study period.

Nonetheless, Mary Lynn and I were scared to death by the prospect of the divisiveness that would be incited, we felt sure, by such an open discussion within the board and the congregation. Introducing the issue, we framed it as a matter of seeking God's will, rather than of finding the majority will of the board. We asked board members what they needed—in terms of both information and process—so that, at the end of our discussion, they could assure themselves that we had done the best job possible of discerning God's will.

They told us they wanted to learn as much as they could about biblical interpretation, especially of those few key passages employed in opposition to the ordination of gays and lesbians. They wanted to learn about the church's tradition on the issue and how that tradition had changed over time. They wanted to hear from these individuals seeking ordination, and to learn how they understood themselves to be called to ministry in the church. They wanted to hear from people on both side of the debate within the church. They wanted to read the most recent scientific literature on what homosexuality is, when it begins, and whether one could ever legitimately call it a "choice." They wanted the opportunity to go slow, to give all board members ample opportunity to say not only what they thought, but also what they felt about the issue. They wanted much input, both rational and spiritual, they said, before they would feel prepared to make such an important decision.

What ensued was a more-than-yearlong process of discernment. Our church board listened to voices on as many sides of the issue as we could identify. We read the work of

researchers who believed homosexuality was a natural phe-
nomenon determined at birth, and of those who believed
that homosexuality was a chosen preference or a psychological illness that could be cured. We read biblical scholars
who were convinced that scripture consistently condemned
same-sex behavior and those who were equally certain that
scripture gave moral standing to covenantal same-sex relationships. We invited local clergy with opposing perspectives on the issue to talk with us. And at every step of the
process, we took time to make sure every board member
had an opportunity to reflect what she or he was hearing
and learning and coming to believe, no matter how long
those conversations took. We regularly invited interested
members of the congregation to talk with us about what they
understood about the issue and to tell us about their own
deepest beliefs.

When the members of the board told Mary Lynn and me
that they were ready to begin making decisions, we prepared
a chart setting out the continuum of actions the board could
take. We set the chart up so that each succeeding point on
the continuum added another layer of affirmation and ac-
ceptance to the one immediately preceding it. The board
members made it clear that they wanted to take an action
that would indicate their affirmation of gay and lesbian
people, so we started our continuum with a first point saying, "We will print a notice in our bulletin each week saying
we welcome people into the full life and ministry of our congregation regardless of their sexual orientation." The second
point included the same statement plus this one: "*and* we
will take steps to communicate our intention to the wider
Davis gay and lesbian community outside the church." Mary
Lynn and I shared the continuum with the board a month
before the date it had set for taking a vote on the issue and
communicating its decision to our denomination's General
Assembly officers. We asked the board to help us refine the
continuum, so that together we identified all the possible
actions we could take and refined the language through
which we described each option.

The next month, the board affirmed its desire to make its decision by consensus. They agreed ahead of time, though, that consensus didn't necessarily require a unanimous vote but a consensus of group spirit. Therefore, Mary Lynn and I decided to proceed through the continuum, asking for an informal show of hands (rather than a formal vote) as the board moved through each point. Board members unanimously supported the first several points along the continuum. Then, for the next several steps the show of hands was 21-1, and then 20-2. When they went to the next position on the continuum, the show of hands was 15-7. Although, by parliamentary rules, that would still be a majority, my intuition told me that we had lost consensus as a community. I checked out my intuition with the board as a whole, and members agreed that consensus had been lost. We went back to the point on the continuum that had garnered the 20-2 vote and asked the two dissenters, "Even though you *personally* disagree with this action, would you be able in good conscience to say that you believe it to be the consensus of session *as a whole*?" Both individuals agreed that they could respond positively to that question, and I offered a prayer of thanksgiving for the consensus that had been reached.

A few months later, both Sandra and I found our interest piqued by an ad in the *Presbyterian Outlook,* an independent church journal. It invited people to a "School for Discernmentarians" led by Chuck Olsen and Danny Morris. Having never heard of either person or his work (much less of the word "discernmentarian"), Sandra and I were curious enough to attend. Olsen and Morris introduced us to the discernment process they had developed.

They explained that they were interested in training "discernmentarians" to help shepherd the discernment process, just as people were trained as parliamentarians to help shepherd a parliamentary process. The most important thing we learned from them was that the process Mary Lynn and I had put together by following our best hunches and intuitions mirrored pretty closely their more formal process for discernment. That confirmation was an important milestone along the way of our congregation's beginning to discern the shape of the emerging church. It taught Sandra and me (and—by extension—the rest of Davis Church's leadership) that trusting our intuitions really *was* a faithful way to move forward into whatever new form of church life was beginning to emerge in our congregation.

While we still used parliamentary procedure to help us make many decisions in our church board, Mary Lynn and I held the reins it provided far more loosely than we once did. We worked hard to make sure that the voices of all got a chance to be heard, even those of the most introverted among us. We stopped far more often in our discussions to ask what voices from scripture or from the wider church we needed to hear, to ask someone to suggest a hymn for us to sing or to lead us in prayer before we moved on. We wove a lot more spaces for silent reflection into our deliberations. We worked hard to try to improve communication between the board and the congregation as a whole, so that all our members knew that their voices, as well, could be heard in our deliberations. And while Mary Lynn and I shared the moderating function for our board, we did everything we could to make it clear that ours were just two voices among many seeking together to discern God's will. We ended each board meeting with a time for speaking the truth in love to one another. We asked board members to speak as honestly and lovingly as they could about moments when they felt the Spirit moving in our meeting and times when it was blocked. We asked them to tell us when they felt they were heard and when they felt shut out from the conversation. We found that not only did this conversation help us all experience an equality around the table; it also helped us surface and resolve hurt feelings that, left unattended, could fester into emotional "disconnects" between board members.

The Davis church board continued to use a more formal process of discernment when board members believed that the issue warranted it. They used it to decide in 2002 whether, in light of our earlier decision to be a congregation that fully welcomed people of all sexual orientations into its life and ministry, we should continue to be the charter organization for three Boy Scout units (we decided we should, despite the national Scouting board's continuing policy banning gay men and boys from Scouting). It helped us make the decision to end our Band-Aid approach to homeless ministry and to wrestle more deeply with what it would mean fully to welcome the homeless into our community's life. Board members recently began a discernment process on whether they should allow wine to be served with meals in church facilities. (While that may not seem to be a major issue to some readers, in a tradition still shaped by the echoes of the temperance movement, I can assure you that it is.) I have learned something unexpected about discernment along the way. Invariably, members of our church board said, in retrospect, that they had felt most faithful and most fully engaged in the ministry of leadership as we were going through the difficult, messy, and sometimes contentious work of discernment. They recommended it with a joy that most of us don't normally associate with serving on a church board. Their response served to solidify my commitment to discernment as a process for church governance.

Recovering a Deeper Pastoral Vocation

In his book *Under the Unpredictable Plant*,[4] retired Regent College professor Eugene Peterson tells about the time earlier in his ministry when he tried to resign from a pastorate. Because he had taken on all the administrative and CEO functions that most American congregations are more than glad to load onto their pastors' shoulders, he was exhausted. Even more critically, he realized he was giving so much of himself to his parish that he was seriously shortchanging his relationships with his family and his own self-care.

In a panic about the state of his spiritual and emotional life, he called a meeting of the church board. Telling the elders he no longer had the time to do the things he thought were most important to his ministry, he submitted his resignation. Rather than taking him up on his offer, though, they asked him what it was he most deeply wanted to do. He told them he wanted to immerse himself in scripture, prayer, reflection, and pastoral conversation with individuals so that he could be the best pastor possible for them. Then what can only be described as a holy moment unfolded.

> One elder said, with some astonishment, "If that is what you want to do, why don't you do it? Nobody told you couldn't, did they?" And I, with a touch of anger, said, "Because I have to run this church. Do you realize that running this church is a full-time job? There is simply no time to be a pastor."
>
> Another elder said, "Why don't you let us run the church?" I said, "You don't know how." He said, "It sounds to me like you don't know how to be a pastor either. How about you let us learn how to run the church and we let you learn how to be a pastor?"[5]

The ironic truth is that our congregations don't *really* want us to be CEOs. They don't really want us to know how to fix the copier or to head the next capital campaign (though they are glad to let us step in and do those things if we're chumps enough to take them on!). What they *really* want is a *pastor*—someone who seeks to draw close to God through the study of scripture, theological reflection, and prayer, and who then seeks to share through preaching, teaching, pastoral care, *and* governance what he or she has discovered. A mentor of mine has suggested that what parishioners really want is for clergy to be pastor-theologians in residence for a local Christian community. When we get in touch with such a deeper definition of our vocation, then even those practical arenas of church life like governance can be reframed, so that we exercise our roles pastorally.

Developing More Communal Polities

The call to wrestle with details of polity might, at first, seem a less important issue in our effort to discern the shape of the emerging church. We typically think of polity as a hidden discipline, of real interest only to pastors, church boards, and judicatory officials. But when we step back a bit, we begin to see how the ways in which we make decisions—whose voices are heard, how broadly the community is consulted (including the community of saints through the ages), and whether our structures concentrate power in the hands of a few—are critical issues for postmodern Christians. They are leery of hierarchical organization charts in which those at the top of the pyramid are the predominant wielders of power. Instead, they value human communities with "flat" organizational structures in which many get to speak and in which many voices are considered for their wisdom. Postmoderns want pastors who bring their particular gifts and training to the congregation's life but who do not control its life. They have a deep desire to belong to a *community* rather than an *organization*. Developing more communal, less formally bureaucratic polities that allow their voices—and everyone else's—to be heard will help make our congregations the kinds of communities they seek.

CHAPTER 7

Beginning to
Learn How to See

The Gospel of Mark tells a compelling story of healing that can help us understand the predicament we face as we seek to discern the shape of the emerging church.

> They came to Bethsaida. Some people brought a blind man to him and begged him to touch him. He took the blind man by the hand and led him out of the village; and when he had put saliva on his eyes and laid his hands on him, he asked him, "Can you see anything?" And the man looked up and said, "I can see people, but they look like trees, walking." Then Jesus laid his hands on his eyes again; and he looked intently and his sight was restored, and he saw everything clearly.
>
> Mark 8:22-25

We have been called to parish ministry in what Loren Mead called "the time between paradigms."[1] Whether we are pre-boomers born before 1945, boomers, gen Xers, or even younger, our blessing and curse is the same. We are pastors during a period when the congregations we serve have one foot in a Christendom era passing from the scene and one foot in the dawning postmodern, post-Christian, and post-denominational world. Even if we serve a congregation that consciously thinks of itself as a "seeker church," we still employ forms of church life developed in the Christendom era. There is, after all, not that much difference between the typical seeker service and the frontier revival service developed in the 19th century. If we serve a congregation in which most folk pine for the "glory days" of the 1950s, others in our church will realize that we need to do something different if the church is going to be faithful into the future.

In this sense, then, we are all like the blind man in Mark's story. We live in that moment between the first and second times Jesus laid hands on him. When we look out at the new American cultural landscape, trying to see what we need to do in response, everything looks blurry, undefined, and frustrating. We want to see clearly. We want Jesus to go ahead and give our eyesight that second touch of healing that will enable us to see clearly. In our hearts, though, we know that it may be some years before we will see as clearly as we would hope. The cultural context for our ministry is shifting so rapidly that we don't have the luxury of waiting till we can see new forms of ministry clearly. We need to start moving into that new landscape while cultural cataracts still blur our vision.

The man in Mark's story, in fact, has an advantage over us. The suggestion that he knows what trees ought to look like has led many interpreters to conclude that this man was not *born* blind. Maybe he lost his sight to disease or illness. Whatever the cause of his blindness, Jesus' healing restores his sight. And when the man opens his eyes, he at least remembers what trees look like and bases his guess about what he's *now* seeing on that memory. But when we look around at the new cultural landscape into which we are moving, it's as though we've been transported to another planet. We recognize almost nothing. The faint outlines we can begin to make out don't remind us of anything we've seen before. And so, at least at first, our attempts to describe what we see won't come even as close as the man's "trees, walking."

Does our impaired sight mean that we're condemned to stumble along into the future, bumping into people and trees alike? Is there something more we can do than read everything on postmodernism we can get our hands on and try to piece together in our heads the individual fragments of the puzzle the authors put into our hands?

I have an additional strategy to offer, one based on the process through which I believe the Spirit has helped me—and the congregation I recently served—to see at least a bit more clearly in our new context for ministry.

Listening More Deeply to the Spirit

I can tell you the moment Mary Lynn, Sandra, and I realized we were being invited into a process of listening to the Spirit more carefully as we exercised leadership in our congregation. Shortly after I began my pastorate, the church board set up a long-range planning committee. It did its work well and submitted a report to the board at the end of its deliberations. We scheduled time on the board's agenda to discuss what to do with the committee's recommendations. But none of the elders seemed to know quite how to proceed. After a couple of months of unsatisfying deliberation, I suggested that the pastoral staff work with the report in the intervening month and come back to the next meeting with suggestions for moving forward.

That next week, the three of us decided our first step would be to go into our individual studies and write a brief narrative about our vision for the congregation's future—where each of us thought God was calling the church to go during the next several years. When we came back together to share what we had written, we were astounded to find that our individual visions were practically identical. "This has to be a gift of the Holy Spirit," one of us said. "There's no way we would see things so similarly if the Spirit weren't drawing us to a common vision."

As a result of that experience, Sandra, Mary Lynn, and I decided to begin spending some time each week praying together. We prayed for the Spirit to deepen the gift of shared vision we had discovered. We prayed for one another and for our individual journeys of faith. We shared what was going on in our lives, where we were experiencing our deepest joys and our deepest pain, both personally and in our roles within the congregation. It was in the context of that covenant to pray with and for one another that we began to sense the leadership of the Spirit more clearly as we, in turn, sought to provide leadership for the congregation.

What surprised us was that as we ourselves began to seek a deeper relationship with God, a similar process of deepening began to take place within the congregation. I don't completely understand that occurrence, but it was clear to us that the two phenomena were intimately connected. Perhaps it was that we began sharing with others what we were discovering about the Spirit's call to each of us. Maybe our ministries took on more depth because of our deepening devotional lives. However one might describe it, the Spirit was able to move more freely through the congregation than before.

Developing an Inductive Field for the Spirit

I developed an image for a theory about what's been happening, a theory I'm still testing out. Imagine that you have a snare drum, but in place of the usual drumhead, you've stretched a sheet of rubber across the top and sides and drawn it taut. If you push down in the center of the rubber sheet with your index finger forcefully enough, the entire drumhead will become a gently sloping cone. If you then place a marble on the outer edge of the drumhead and give it even the slightest nudge, it will spiral down into that depression your finger has created.

I believe an analogous process begins when a few key leaders in a congregation covenant with one another to begin asking the Holy Spirit to help them grow in faith. Their shared commitment to go deeper in their own spiritual pilgrimage (the finger pushing down in the center) opens a way for God to begin to invite all members of the congregation to go deeper in *their* spiritual journeys (the slope that pulls the marble down to the deepest point of the cone). It enables people to sense more readily the nudges of the Spirit that can, in turn, draw them more deeply into their relationships with the Triune God. It was out of our own commitment to go deeper that Mary Lynn and I developed the courage and the faith in our hunches to step out in faith into the future. We discovered we were more willing to risk experimenting with new forms of ministry—forms our intuitions told us would be more faithful in the emerging cultural context into which God was calling us. We were encouraged to risk failure as well as success, because we could trust that it was the Spirit helping us to see more clearly, as we move into that future, what God has in mind for us.

In his conversation with the Twelve just before his death, Jesus—according to John's Gospel—promises his followers, "I will not leave you orphaned" (John 14:18). It might help us more in our present situation to hear his words in an older translation, "I will not leave you comfortless" (KJV). Even though the disciples do not yet fully understand, they are standing on the cusp between two worlds as Jesus speaks these words. They are teetering between the world of love and comfort they have known in Jesus' presence and the world of terror they will enter after his death.

Knowing that the disciples are on the brink of having to learn to see the world all over again, Jesus promises them the gift of the Holy Spirit—the comforter and the guide to all truth. Jesus promises that the Spirit will give them new vision to see this new world rightly. The Spirit will help them discover the skills they need to navigate successfully through this new world. The Spirit will help them form a new community that will faithfully incarnate the mission of Jesus in its own life and bear that mission into an alien landscape.

While the shift in cultural contexts we are now living through is not nearly as stark as what the disciples experienced following Jesus' death and resurrection, still there are times when we feel comfortless. We, too, are being asked to see a new world rightly.

Jesus' promise to us is the same as it was to his first disciples. He promises us the gift of the Holy Spirit, to support and encourage us as we step out in faith into our own new context for ministry. The Spirit will, in our own time, help us form a new community that will faithfully bear the mission of Jesus in the postmodern, post-Christian, post-denominational world.

Take the Next Step

If you want to set out on this journey with a new sense of purpose and desire to be more faithful to God's call, then I urge you to establish a covenant group of leaders in your congregation. Whether or not they are the formally elected leaders, bring together a small group of people you sense are beginning to hear the call of the Spirit to enter this new cultural landscape in faith. Invite them to enter with you into a prayerful process of opening yourselves to the guidance of the Spirit about how to minister in the emerging cultural context. Ask each person to talk about what she or he can already sense about the new world in which we live and how the Spirit might be inviting the community to respond.

Start to share your emerging vision with your church board and other leaders in your congregation. Ask them to step out in faith with you and risk new forms of ministry that your Spirit-guided intuition tells you may be more appropriate in a postmodern, post-Christian context. Your hunches won't always be on target, but don't fear failure. There really is no other way forward right now, and you will learn as much from your failures as you will from your successes.

Find colleagues in other congregations who are on the same journey of exploration, both within your own tradition and across denominational lines. Share stories about what you're learning as you seek to follow the Spirit's leading. Listen for new insights developed in other congregations. Help each other describe more accurately both the new cultural context into which we are moving and what seems to be the most faithful response to that context.

The Joy of Faithful Exploration

We do live in a time between paradigms, a time when we look into the future of the church and can see only dimly and faintly. But what an exciting time to be involved in ministry! No plodding along for us, doing what we've always comfortably done before. We are invited by the Spirit to be pioneers in a postmodern frontier and to step out in faith and reliance on the Spirit's guidance as we seek to be faithful in a landscape where many of our old road maps are useless. We are, to paraphrase the opening of every "Star Trek" television episode, invited to go boldly where no church has gone before. As we trust in Christ's promises that we will not be left comfortless but will be led into that future by the Holy Spirit, we will experience a deep joy as we begin to discern the features of the emerging church.

NOTES

Chapter 1
1. Diogenes Allen, "The End of the Modern World" (Princeton, N.J.: pamphlet produced by the Center of Theological Inquiry, 1994), 6–10.
2. Glenn Tinder, "Can We Be Good Without God?" *The Atlantic Monthly* 264, no. 6 (December 1989): 69–85.

Chapter 2
1. Martin B. Copenhaver, Anthony B. Robinson, and William H. Willimon, *Good News in Exile: Three Pastors Offer a Hopeful Vision for the Church* (Grand Rapids: Eerdmans, 1999), 24.
2. For example, see Darrell L. Guder, ed., *Missional Church: A Vision for the Sending of the Church in North America* (Grand Rapids: Eerdmans, 1998).

Chapter 4
1. William Placher, "Is the Bible True?," *The Christian Century*, October 11, 1995, 924f.

Chapter 5
1. Loren B. Mead, *The Once and Future Church: Reinventing the Congregation for a New Mission Frontier* (Washington, D.C.: Alban Institute, 1991).
2. Mead, *Once and Future Church*, 22.

3. Darrell L. Guder, ed., *Missional Church: A Vision for the Sending of the Church in North America* (Grand Rapids: Eerdmans, 1998), 4.
4. Guder, *Missional Church*, 109.

Chapter 6
1. See Stanley Hauerwas and William H. Willimon, *Resident Aliens: Life in the Christian Colony* (Nashville: Abingdon, 1989) and *Where Resident Aliens Live: Exercises for Christian Practice* (Nashville: Abingdon, 1996).
2. See Charles M. Olsen, *Transforming Church Boards into Communities of Spiritual Leaders* (Bethesda, Md.: Alban Institute, 1995), and Danny E. Morris and Charles M. Olsen, *Discerning God's Will Together: A Spiritual Practice for the Church* (Bethesda, Md.: Alban Institute, 1997).
3. Luke Timothy Johnson, *Scripture and Discernment: Decision Making in the Church* (Nashville: Abingdon, 1983).
4. Eugene H. Peterson, *Under the Unpredictable Plant: An Exploration in Vocational Holiness* (Grand Rapids: Eerdmans, 1992).
5. Peterson, *Unpredictable Plant*, 39.

Chapter 7
1. Loren B. Mead, *The Once and Future Church: Reinventing the Congregation for a New Mission Frontier* (Washington, D.C.: Alban Institute, 1991), 22.